ON EAGLE'S WINGS

MICHAEL JONCAS

On
Eagle's
Wings

A Journey through
Illness toward Healing

**TWENTY-THIRD
PUBLICATIONS**
twentythirdpublications.com

TWENTY-THIRD PUBLICATIONS
One Montauk Avenue, Suite 200
New London, CT 06320
(860) 437-3012 or (800) 321-0411
www.twentythirdpublications.com

Cover photo: ©Superstock / Blend Images / Blend Images

ISBN: 978-1-62785-215-9
Library of Congress Control Number: 2017945076
Printed in the U.S.A.

 A Division of Bayard, Inc.

CONTENTS

INTRODUCTION

I never expected to write a book like this. My other books have been primarily academic, dealing with worship or musical issues. This book is much more personal, a combination of journal entries, later reflections on the events I record, and the memories of family and friends who walked with me through a year of sickness, suffering, and recovery.

From April 2003 to June 2004 my usual life of preaching and presiding at liturgy, teaching, researching, composing, and offering presentations in various venues was shattered. I was ensnared in a neurological disorder, eventually diagnosed as Guillain-Barré Syndrome (GBS). Grappling with this disorder led to three months of hospitalization at St. Mary's Hospital, part of the Mayo Clinic in Rochester, MN; another three months of outpatient therapy at Bethesda Rehabilitation Hospital in St. Paul, MN; and six months of home therapy before returning to my priestly and academic responsibilities.

In the years since, I have had the chance to reflect rather deeply on this time. I believe that what I underwent can be mapped and described in five stages that the following pages will outline. I do not claim that this structure will be true for all sufferers, but I believe nonetheless that exploring these stages might be helpful for others experiencing their own time of suffering and for those who care for them.

Many of my readers probably know that I have spent some forty years writing and promoting church music for the revised Roman Rite Catholic liturgy. As will become clear in my narrative, I couldn't create any new compositions during my time of affliction, and I continued to be creatively blocked for nearly two years after coming down with GBS. However, in October 2005, it was as though the floodgates opened and I wrote a significant number of compositions in a short period of time. Listening to the new compositions, I detected not only a change in my compositional style but (at least in my opinion) a deepening in the compositions themselves. I now believe that some of these compositions arose as I was undergoing the stages of suffering I will describe. So I conclude each chapter with some suggested listening, one composition created in the period after my time with GBS that I believe expresses in some way the experience of the particular stage I had faced.

I offer these reflections in thanksgiving to the medical personnel who helped me confront GBS, to my family and friends who stood by me through my hospitalization and recovery, and to God, who has walked with me through the valley of the shadow of death and opened new ways of ministering for me. If God uses these reflections to touch the hearts of any of my readers with his healing grace, I will be delighted and enriched.

I would especially like to thank Frs. George Szews, Kevin McDonough, Tom Kommers, and also Vicki Klima and my family members for sharing their memories and thoughts about the events I've described. Without their observations this book could never have been written.

Finally I express particular gratitude to all those who helped to bring this book into being: Therese Ratliff, PhD, publisher at Twenty-Third Publications, for accepting the manuscript; Dan Connors, editorial director at Twenty-Third Publications, who worked tirelessly at turning the manuscript into a book; Jeff McCall, who created the cover; and Patricia "Trish" Vanni, who encouraged me to bring this project to Twenty-Third Publications and who has encouraged me in its creation.

As Johann Sebastian Bach was accustomed to write on his completed musical scores: "Soli Deo gloria" (To God alone be the glory).

CHAPTER ONE

Chaos and Confusion

B efore beginning the narrative of my transformative encounter with GBS, I'd like to give you some background on my life up to 2003. These biographical notes are by no means complete, but should still give you a sense of the disruption GBS brought into my life and how profoundly it changed me.

BACKGROUND

I was born in Minneapolis, MN, in 1951, the son of Paul Eugene Joncas and Theresa Janine (Narog) Joncas. My dad worked in a variety of settings associated with the performing arts: as a set designer, floor manager, and makeup man for Twin Cities television companies (KSTP, WCCO, KTCA); as a stagehand for professional troupes who came to perform in our area; and eventually as a teacher of theater arts at the University of Minnesota. He spent his free time whittling and painting watercolors and oils. My mom was a long-term medical secretary for the Hennepin County pathology department, but she had also taken voice lessons starting in high school and sang both semi-professionally and around the house. I attribute my permanent love of the arts and long-term avocation as a composer of church music to their influence.

I was also blessed by coming from a large family, the eldest of eight children. I will list them here in order of birth, so that when they appear later in the narrative you'll have some sense of who they are: Jeanine Marie (born 1953), Kathleen Rose (born 1956), Babette Anne (born 1958), Patrice Clare (born 1960), Stacie Lee (born 1961), Joseph Paul (born 1963) and Kim Marie (born 1966). All were alive during my bout with GBS with the exception of Babette, who had died in her twenties, felled by a form of epilepsy that stopped her heart during a major seizure.

I am the product of long Catholic schooling, attending St. Lawrence Catholic School in southeast Minneapolis until third grade and then moving to northeast Minneapolis, where I attended St. Charles Borromeo Catholic school. Discerning a possible call to the priesthood after eighth grade, I attended Nazareth Hall, the preparatory seminary for the Archdiocese of St. Paul and Minneapolis, from 1965–1969, and the University of St. Thomas as part of St. John Vianney College Seminary from 1969–1973, graduating with a B.A. in English. After working at St. Joseph's Parish in New Hope, MN, as a liturgy and music director for three years, I returned to the diocesan major seminary, the St. Paul Seminary, and was ordained for the Archdiocese as a diocesan priest in 1980.

After ordination I served as assistant pastor at Presentation of the Blessed Virgin Mary parish on the east side of St. Paul for four years, and then as education coordinator and campus minister at our Newman Center at the University of Minnesota (Twin Cities) for three years. I had already earned a M.A. in theology, specializing in liturgical studies, from the University of Notre Dame in Indiana during the summers I worked at St. Joseph's, so when I had the opportunity to complete my education in liturgy, I jumped at the chance. Archbishop John Roach sent me to the Pontificio Instituto Liturgico of the Ateneo Sant'Anselmo in Rome, where I earned an S.L.L. (licenciate in Sacred Liturgy) and S.L.D. (doctorate in Sacred Liturgy). When I returned home, I began full-time teaching in the Department of Theology at the University of Thomas. The "powers that be" at St. Thomas have always been remarkably kind to me, allowing me to teach for various lengths of time at other institutions of higher learning such as the Angelicum in Rome, St. John's University in Collegeville, MN, and at the University of Notre Dame in Indiana, where for nearly a decade I taught in the summer school program of liturgical studies and during the spring semester of odd-numbered years in the Department of Theology. It was in the spring of 2003 that my adventure with GBS began.

THE STORY

17 April 2003   *Holy Thursday*

I think I first suspected that something out of the ordinary was happening to me as I celebrated the Holy Thursday liturgy with the Sisters of the Holy Cross on 17 April 2003. I had developed a warm relationship with the sisters at St. Mary's College (the "sister" school to Notre Dame) and they frequently invited me to preside and preach for Sunday Eucharist in their magnificent college chapel. So I was honored and delighted when they invited me to preside and preach at the Holy Thursday Evening Mass of the Lord's Supper. Faithful to their Catholic heritage, Notre Dame and St. Mary's designated the time of the Easter Triduum (Holy Thursday through Easter Sunday) and Easter Monday as holidays, so I was looking forward both to some time of intense prayer and of relaxation from classroom teaching before the final push of the semester.

The first sign I noticed that something was "off" occurred as I sweat through the Holy Thursday vestments with an intensity that was visible to members of the community who had gathered to pray. I sweat quite easily (a genetic gift from my father, I believe, who was also a large man), but never before had I concluded a liturgy realizing I had soaked my underwear, my shirt and pants, and the alb, stole, and chasuble (an undergarment, a badge of office, and a flowing overgarment that are part of the prescribed vestments for a priest celebrating Mass in the Roman Rite). Long after I came back to health, members of the St. Mary's community present at this Holy Thursday liturgy told me how puzzled they were seeing me sweat so copiously when the ambient temperature was springlike, if not chilly.

More concerning to me was the awareness that I couldn't raise the chalice and paten (the wine cup and bread plate used at Eucharist) to where I would usually elevate them at the conclusion of the Eucharistic prayer (the central prayer of praise and thanksgiving from which Eucharist takes its name: the Greek word *eucharistia* = thanksgiving). While I noted the experience, I thought I was simply experiencing some muscle weakness. I had been teaching with my usual intensity the whole semester and judged that I was just tired and that any muscular weakness I felt would disappear after a good night's rest.

I know now that I must have surmised that these symptoms were more serious than I suspected, because I called both my mother and my sister Kathy to wish them a Happy Easter (trusting that they would pass my good wishes on to my other relatives) and reported what I had experienced.

Thinking that they were being supportive and having no reason to believe that there was anything serious about my symptoms since I had always been a healthy guy, they agreed with me that a good night's sleep would probably bring me back to shipshape.

18 April 2003   *Good Friday*

However, I had further confirmation that something odd was transpiring when, in spite of the fact that I was exhausted from celebrating the liturgy at St. Mary's, I only slept in fits and starts that night. New symptoms appeared: it became physically harder and harder to get up from my bed; walking into the bathroom in bare feet became grueling due to the strange sensations I was feeling on the bottoms of my feet (as though I had Brillo pads attached to them); and a weird weakness took over my right arm (though I thought at this stage that the weakness was the result of too much grading of undergraduate essays yoked to sleeping on the arm in a way that hurt the muscles). I tried to tell myself that these were just passing difficulties and that if I could only get a good night's sleep things would be fine. Although I had planned to attend the Good Friday liturgy at St. Mary's, I gave myself permission to take an afternoon nap instead, thinking that I would attend an evening liturgy in a local parish in lieu of the afternoon liturgy.

I didn't really worry until I tried to prepare supper for myself that evening. (Adult Roman Catholics of the Roman

Rite between the ages of fourteen and sixty observe "fasting and abstinence" on Good Friday, i.e., limit their eating to one full meatless meal [with the possibility of two other small meals that do not together constitute a full meal] on the day that commemorates Jesus' death; the obligation to abstain from meat holds from age fourteen on). I could not work the can opener nor could I lift the cooking pots from the cupboard to the stovetop burners. Clearly this was more than a passing difficulty.

So I called the clinic at Notre Dame, hoping that there'd be someone on call even though the University was shut down for the Triduum weekend. Surprisingly a nurse associated with the university clinic called me back but said that the regular on-call doctor was gone for the holiday weekend and that I should go to a local hospital if I felt I needed more care. I assured her that, while I was concerned about my symptoms, I didn't feel they were serious enough to "bother" the doctors at one of South Bend's hospitals.

I described some of my symptoms to Fr. Michael Driscoll, a good friend and a colleague in liturgical studies at Notre Dame, and asked him for a recommendation for medical care. He kindly offered to try to get his own personal physician to care for me, but I told Michael I didn't want to bother his medical caretaker, especially on a holiday weekend. I asked Michael to direct me to whatever institutions would be available in the South Bend area that also had a reputation for good medical practice. Michael directed me to an Urgent Care clinic not far from the University campus.

I also called my best priest friend, Fr. George Szews, at that time pastor of the Newman community in Eau Claire, WI, to get his advice on what I should do. He agreed with Michael Driscoll that I should try to a get professional medical opinion about what was going on with me, but left the decision about when to do so up to me.

Even though it was now the time when I had intended to participate in the local parish's evening Liturgy of the Lord's Passion, I felt that I should get to Urgent Care as quickly as possible. Unfortunately, when I finally found the address and reached the clinic, they had closed for the day. The notice on the door said that they'd reopen at 7 AM on Saturday, so I decided that I'd be there bright and early the next morning.

19 April 2003   *Holy Saturday*

The night between Good Friday and Holy Saturday repeated the pattern from Holy Thursday to Good Friday, i.e., I barely slept more than fifteen minutes at a time and my muscular deterioration continued. My legs and feet grew increasingly weak overnight, so that getting out of bed was becoming more and more difficult. I started to wonder whether, if my legs and feet continued in the direction they were going, I would be able to drive myself to Urgent Care.

I drove from the residence Notre Dame had provided for me during the semester so as to arrive at the recommended Urgent Care right when it opened at 7 AM on

Holy Saturday morning. I was met at the desk by a nurse-receptionist who asked me why I was there. She also asked me to fill out the inevitable forms providing both a partial picture of my health to that point and an indication that I would be able to pay whatever charges I might accrue. Since there was no one else in the office she rather quickly ushered me in to get a diagnosis from the doctor in charge.

I honestly don't remember my physical exam, but I remember the doctor taking what seemed like a long time with me. He had a very soothing demeanor and was successful in calming my mounting anxiety. After at least an hour's exam the doctor said that I was suffering from a "bad case of nerves," probably brought on by too much intense teaching that semester. Since the first real break occurred over the Easter holiday my psyche had given my body permission to signal that I needed some extensive rest and relaxation. He told me to go home, get some sleep, and if the symptoms persisted over the next week or so to get back in touch.

I felt greatly relieved at what he had told me. I immediately drove home and went to bed, trying to make up for the sleep I had lost the last two evenings as well as preparing to attend the evening Easter Vigil later that evening. (The Roman Rite Easter Vigil consists of a lengthy church service begun after sunset and concluded before dawn. It consists of: 1) a light service in which the Easter fire is kindled, the Paschal Candle lit and processed through a darkened church as the participants light their own candles from the Paschal Candle, and a lengthy chant in praise of the candle and its light as symbols of the triumph of Christ over the powers of darkness; 2) a lengthy vigil consisting of up to seven Old Testament readings with their corresponding psalms and prayers; 3) the Liturgy of the Word from the Easter Mass involving the singing of the "Glory to God," the reading of the Epistle, the singing of an Easter Sequence and the Gospel Alleluia, and the solemn proclamation of the Gospel by deacon or priest, followed by the Easter homily; 4) water rites ranging from full initiation of the unbaptized elect through reception of the baptized into the communion of the Catholic Church to a question-and-answer form of the Creed, depending on whether the local community is welcoming new adult members at the Vigil or not; and finally 5) the Easter Liturgy of the Eucharist.)

The same pattern of interrupted sleep I had experienced from Holy Thursday on lasted throughout the day on Holy Saturday. When I finally gave up on trying to rest, I discovered that, rather than regaining some of my muscular control, if anything my muscles had deteriorated since I had seen the doctor that morning. I was starting to panic. I kept moving from bed to bathroom to chair to walking in the apartment in a circle to try and determine for myself if my responses were improving, maintaining, or declining. It became clear to me by late afternoon that I would not be able to attend the Easter Vigil (an incredible disappointment for me as it is the high point of the liturgical year and I had attended it faithfully every year from grade-school on) and that I should get a second opinion on the diagnosis I was given.

Unfortunately, by the time I made that decision the Urgent Care I had gone to was closed, but I had checked that it would reopen for business at 7 AM on Easter Sunday. I planned to return to Urgent Care as soon as its doors opened the next day.

20 April 2003   *Easter Sunday*

After another fairly sleepless night in which my muscular deterioration had seemed to me to have plateaued, I called my friend George, very worried because I found while dressing myself that morning it was difficult for me to button my shirt. I'm fairly sure I had been negotiating that task since I was about three years old, and I grew impatient (and scared) when the simple task of getting a button through the appropriate buttonhole took more and more time. George told me to call 911 immediately, but I thought I should continue the plan I had decided on the night before and drove to the same Urgent Care I had visited earlier as it opened bright and early at 7 AM. It was at this point that an event occurred that I interpret as manifesting the providence of God through human intervention.

The same nurse-receptionist was behind the desk when I again asked to see a doctor. She recognized me from the day before (although I'm sure she would have made the connection when I filled out the necessary paperwork for this new visit). She asked: "Didn't you come here yesterday with a complaint about progressive muscular weakness?" When I confirmed her memory she said in a voice that had suddenly become quiet and confidential: "Please don't report this to anyone because I could lose my job over telling you, but I strongly believe that we don't have the personnel or the technology to diagnose whatever you may have." After I had assured her that I would not repeat what she had told me, I asked what she recommended. She said that I should immediately drive myself to the emergency room of one of the major hospitals in South Bend. I thanked her for her honesty and said that I would follow her suggestion.

While some readers might judge that the nurse-receptionist was out of line for telling me that the Urgent Care I had visited was not able to deal with my symptoms, while others might see her concern for me as a patient properly manifested in what she told me, I actually thank God for her intervention. I believe that in some mysterious way God worked through her own professional ethics to set me on a road that would eventually lead to my healing, even at the possible price of losing her job.

(In case a reader might wonder whether I am breaking my promise to her by writing about this incident in this book, you should know that she never told me her name nor do I remember that she wore a name tag or that her name appeared by the desk at which she was stationed. I have also been careful not to reveal what Urgent Care I went to so I believe her identity can't be traced. In fact when I returned to South Bend a few years later, I tried to look her up to thank her but was unsuccessful. I keep her in my prayers of gratitude.)

Following the nurse-receptionist's advice, I drove to one of the hospitals, parked my car, and after filling out another raft of paperwork, was admitted for observation and diagnosis. (In the light of what I will recount of my time there in this and the next chapter, I am likewise not revealing the identity of this hospital or its personnel.) However, I neglected to tell anyone either at Notre Dame or back home what I was doing or where I was. George got the assistance of a young doctor, Kevin Henseler, who had been a student in George's parish and was now practicing in the Twin Cities, to find out in which South Bend hospital I was. Kevin was able to determine to which hospital I had been admitted, but didn't have any further information about my condition.

I had been assigned a bed in a two-person room with an elderly man suffering from Alzheimer's disease who yelled incomprehensible phrases at unpredictable intervals. To keep him from disturbing the rest of the ward, hospital personnel closed the door to our room, which meant that they also didn't check on me from the time I was admitted as far as I could tell. (I was to learn quickly that hospitals tend to be noisy places where it is difficult to sleep for any length of time in one period; I do know that I didn't sleep at all Easter Sunday night.) Later that afternoon I lost the use of my legs, being unable to get out of bed without human assistance or walk for any length of time without a walker or cane.

Once again I felt that I had experienced God's providence insofar as my legs did not give out while I was driving. I imagined what might have happened to me and to any people who might have unfortunately been in my way if the leg-weakness had kicked in while I was on the road. But I also became convinced how serious my condition was becoming, because the paralysis had come on so quickly; without a diagnosis, I didn't know what was happening to me or what I could expect.

Meanwhile, George and Vicki Klima, the then-director of the Worship Center for the Archdiocese of St. Paul and Minneapolis, were celebrating the conclusion of the complex and lengthy services of Triduum in their communities by having a festive dinner at the St. Paul Hotel. I fear I spoiled their much-deserved celebration since the conversation focused on whether or not they should immediately visit me in the hospital in South Bend. Apparently they rather quickly decided to do so and checked for flights. Unfortunately there were no flights scheduled for Easter Monday that would get them to the hospital in a timely fashion, so they decided to drive. Knowing that they were both exhausted from their liturgical responsibilities, they enlisted Perry Koeppen, a student at the University of Wisconsin, Menomonie, to see if he'd be willing to drive them overnight to South Bend. He agreed and met them at a parking lot in that city to begin the journey.

REFLECTIONS

I have titled this chapter "Chaos and Confusion" both because it is an accurate description of what I experienced as my illness began and because I identify this state of mind and soul as a usual first stage in confronting major loss and illness. What have I learned through this experience?

I think most of us develop a "default" position from which to analyze our physical, emotional, cognitive, and spiritual status. We identify this customary status as "normal." We tend not to reflect on the extraordinary fact that we exist at all, that we are sustained in being by a Power beyond ourselves, that our various systems synchronize amazingly well. When one or more of the systems departs from what we consider "normal," we react with varying degrees of discomfort all the way to panic and dread. In my case I discovered that, although my religious tradition and priestly practice directed me to live in gratitude (viz., the stereotyped opening of many of the Prefaces that priests pray at the opening the Eucharistic Prayer in the Roman Rite: "It is truly right and just, our duty and our salvation, always and everywhere to give you thanks, Lord, holy Father, almighty and eternal God…"), I was not, in fact, a very grateful person. Rather I demanded that God manifest his care for me in a direct and, as far as possible, immediate way. My petitions for healing were utterly self-centered and mostly consisted in bargaining with God to let me return to what I considered "normal."

I don't judge myself harshly today for not having a more noble reaction to the onset of my illness, but I hope I have learned something. Now, rather than immediately judging new sensations as "abnormal," I try to observe them dispassionately. Most importantly, I try to cultivate gratefulness "always and everywhere," so that I can honestly say "thank you" to God for the beauty of a summer day *and* for the harsh chill of winter, for success in communicating through a classroom lecture *and* for the disasters that come from trying new teaching techniques, for the friends who sustain me *and* the friends who challenge me. As the young curate comes to know by the end of Georges Bernanos' magnificent novel *Diary of a Country Priest*: "All is grace."

Suggested Listening

As I wrote in the introduction, my experience of GBS profoundly affected all the aspects of my life, including my creative compositional work. It was only after some years of recovery that I was able to compose again. I have chosen five of the compositions I completed after coming down with GBS as suggested listening for the conclusion of each chapter. I believe my experience of "chaos and confusion" deeply informs my setting of Psalm 104, "Lord Send Out Your Spirit."

Many of the settings of Psalm 104 are quite jubilant, even rollicking, frequently in triple rhythm. They praise the God who has already answered the pleas of the psalmist, renewing the face of the earth. In contrast my setting, in 6/8 meter, is in a minor key. The antiphon, accompanied by harp and string quartet, almost obsessively centers on the dominant note and a semi-tone above. The sense conveyed is that the earth (and the psalmist) are anything but renewed, in fact are in desperate need of God's intervention and care. The verses are sung *a cappella* by the choir, each verse conveying a particular nuance of the experience of chaos and confusion. The first verse recalls that God has manifested his concern for his creation by filling the earth with his creatures, while the second verse notes just how fragile these creatures (including humans) are. The cut-off quality of the singing on the word "breath" emphasizes that without a steady stream of air filling our lungs we will quickly become a corpse. This terrifying truth came home to me later in my GBS ordeal when the muscles that controlled my breathing collapsed and I was put on a ventilator; my life now literally depended on the constant pulsing of a machine, and I had no control over the mechanics of the ventilator machine or its supply of electricity. The final verse depicts the only act of faith that I could muster in the time of chaos and confusion, that at some future date I *will* again "be glad in the LORD," since I was certainly feeling no joy in my present circumstances.

Refrain: *Lord, send out your Spirit, and renew the face of the earth* (2x)

1. Bless the Lord, O my soul,
   O Lord, my God, you are great indeed!
   How manifold are your works, O Lord!
   The earth is full of your creatures.

2. If you take away their breath they perish
   And return to their dust.
   When you send forth your spirit, they are created,
   And you renew the face of the earth.

3. May the glory of the Lord endure forever;
   May the Lord be glad in his works!
   Pleasing to him be my theme;
   I will be glad in the Lord.

From the GIA CD-207 "In the Sight of the Angels" copyright ©2007. Copies of this CD and sheet music are available through the GIA website (www.giamusic.com) or at GIA Publications, Inc., 7404 S. Mason Avenue, Chicago, IL 60638.

A recorded version of the composition may be accessed at **www.youtube.com/ watch?v=RH3vvmjl3iA**

CHAPTER TWO

Diagnosis

THE STORY

21 April 2003   *Easter Monday*

As I already mentioned, I got no sleep at all Easter Sunday night, but I was surprised, relieved, and deeply heartened to see George, Vicki, and Perry at my bedside at about 5:15 AM on Easter Monday. Overnight, my muscular deterioration had continued. By the time my visitors met me Monday morning, I was unable to raise my hands or arms to the vicinity of my face. Hospital personnel hadn't opened the door overnight because of the outbursts of my roommate. Thus I had no one to assist me to the bathroom, with the result that when George, Vicki, and Perry first saw me I was lying in my own urine. Hospital personnel had left a food tray for me, but since no one was assigned to help me eat, I never touched the tray. I don't remember being especially concerned about that since I wasn't very hungry, but it certainly signaled some real issues about my care.

Later in the day the hospital initiated the process of diagnosis. They sent a wheelchair to transport me to get a magnetic resonance imaging (MRI) scan, a non-invasive medical test using a powerful magnetic field, radio frequency pulses, and a computer to produce detailed pictures of organs, soft tissues, bone, and virtually all other internal body structures. Unfortunately, the MRI of my head and neck areas showed nothing unusual, so the test didn't advance the diagnosis. Perhaps more unfortunately, the hospital personnel associated with this trip only pushed my wheelchair but wouldn't transfer me from bed to wheelchair and vice versa. As the nurse remarked to George as she pushed my wheelchair at him when I returned from the MRI, "He's way too big for me; you're gonna have to get him out of the wheelchair and into bed." This infuriated George, who immediately went to the nurses' station and pounded on the desk. The chief resident was doing rounds, but came up to the station immediately and asked what was wrong. George told him that he and my other visitors had found me covered in urine when they first arrived that morning because no one had checked on me during the night. George then told the story of the nurse pushing me in a wheelchair toward him and telling him to get me into bed himself. The chief resident made the excuse that it was a holiday weekend and the hospital was short-staffed, but within an hour I was moved from my initial room into a VIP suite.

It was clear that my visitors had now assumed the role of my advocates. By consulting with other friends in the medical field (this was before WebMD and other informative websites on the internet), they educated themselves on what procedures might be done to diagnose my condition. When George met with the head of neurology to ask when electromyography tests (EMG) and nerve conduction studies (NCS) (described in more detail below) would be done on me, the chief neurologist said that he would not order these tests, noting that he was the doctor and that George didn't know what he was talking about. Instead the chief neurologist ordered that I be put on steroids.

A truly comforting prayer service enriched Easter Monday evening. Even though it was a holiday at Notre Dame, my colleague Fr. Michael Driscoll came to my hospital room in the early evening to celebrate the anointing of the sick. As a priest for more than twenty years in 2003, I had celebrated this sacrament with hundreds, if not thousands, of the sick and the suffering over the years. But nothing prepared me for the emotional impact of hearing Fr. Michael address me directly with the following ritual prayer: "Father in heaven, through this holy anointing grant Michael comfort in his suffering. When he is afraid, give him courage; when afflicted, give him patience; when dejected, afford him hope, and when alone assure him of the support of your holy people. We ask this through Christ our Lord. Amen." The prayer brought tears to my eyes, not tears of sadness but tears in response to God's love being mediated to me by Fr. Michael's gestures and texts and those of my friends who were in the hospital room.

The head of the neurology department came to my room later that evening to share with me and my friends what he thought possible diagnoses were. He said that the least likely, but possible, diagnosis was multiple sclerosis (MS). This is a progressive disease of the central nervous system that disrupts the flow of information within the brain and between the brain and the body. Unfortunately MS is difficult to diagnose because the symptoms vary and can change over time, so much so that no two persons have exactly the same symptoms. (My cousin, Rev. Paul Joncas, a Lutheran minister, has had to give up his formal clerical ministry after having been diagnosed with MS, which has progressed to a debilitating stage in his life. This led me to wonder if I, too, sharing a genetic heritage with Paul, might likewise have MS.) A more likely diagnosis was Guillain-Barré Syndrome (GBS), a rare autoimmune disorder in which the body's immune system mistakenly attacks the myelin insulation of the peripheral nerves. Although the rapid-onset muscular weakness I had experienced could signal this condition, there was no single test that could positively identify GBS; rather, after one had excluded other alternative causes, GBS could be the diagnosis of last resort.

(I will describe GBS in more detail in the next chapter.) However the chief neurologist believed that I had transverse myelitis (TM), an inflammation/lesion of the spinal cord damaging nerve fibers and causing them (as in GBS) to lose their myelin coating. Steroids are often given in high doses when symptoms begin in the hope of decreasing the degree of inflammation and swelling of the spinal cord. One-third of people with TM experience full recovery, one-third exhibit fair recovery but may have significant deficits, and the final third experience no recovery at all.

I think the chief neurologist's visit was difficult for me and my friends to process. We had hoped that there would be a swift diagnosis followed by appropriate treatment and that I would leave the hospital and return to teaching to complete the semester at Notre Dame. It was clear that the chief neurologist believed I had TM, since he had ordered me put on steroids. However, my friends looked up the three medical conditions the chief neurologist had mentioned to see how they matched up with my symptoms and to contemplate my future in case I was afflicted with any of them. George renewed his request that the chief neurologist order EMG and NCS tests as an aid to diagnosis and the chief neurologist reluctantly agreed, assigning a staff neurologist to conduct the examinations early the next day. A real blessing was that I was finally able to sleep Monday night after an exhausting day.

Easter Tuesday brought with it the new series of tests measuring muscle response or electrical activity in response to nerve stimulation of a muscle, both electromyography exams (EMG) and nerve conduction studies (NCS). These studies were conducted by a staff neurologist inserting needles into the muscles of my hands, arms, feet, and legs. An EMG measures electrical activity in a resting muscle, during slight contraction of the muscle, and during a more forceful contraction. An NCS, used to determine nerve damage and/or destruction, measures the amount and speed of conduction of an electrical impulse through a nerve. I believe the original plan was to perform the same set of tests on both sides of my body, but after completing the set on one side, the staff neurologist said that he was 90% certain that I had GBS and that I should be started on intravenous immunoglobulin therapy (IVIg) immediately. (I will discuss IVIg treatments in the next chapter.) He also said that it was likely that I would get better, given my age and general health.

I was returned to my room at 8 AM. When no IVIg treatment was started by noon, George had the chief neurologist paged with no response. George continued to have him paged every hour on the hour for the rest of the day, again with no response.

Later that day I experienced a lumbar puncture (sometimes called a spinal tap), a procedure to collect and examine the cerebrospinal fluid (CSF) surrounding the brain and the spinal cord. Although I had heard horror stories about the pain associated with spinal taps and the discomfort involved in remaining perfectly still for a significant amount of time after the lumbar puncture had been completed, the most pain I experienced was from the insertion of the needle with some numbing medicine into my lower back.

While I spent most of Easter Tuesday undergoing these tests, two other good friends, both from the Twin Cities, flew into South Bend to visit me. Fr. Kevin McDonough was at that time the chancellor and vicar general for the Archdiocese of St. Paul and Minneapolis. Fr. Tom Kommers was serving as the founding pastor of St. Thomas Becket parish in Eagan, MN, and preparing to assume the pastorate at St. Joseph's in Red Wing, MN. Kevin, Tom, and I had bonded during the four years we studied as seminarians at the major seminary for our Archdiocese, the St. Paul Seminary in St. Paul. We had formed a priest support group during our time there, and that fraternal support was something we had all come to cherish since being ordained and entering into full-time ministry. They had planned to come to visit me at Notre Dame for a mini-vacation after their Easter liturgical responsibilities and decided not to change their plans when they found out I had been hospitalized. Vicki picked them up at the South Bend airport and they soon found their way to my bedside.

At 6 PM the chief neurologist visited my room to say

that no matter what the staff neurologist had told us, he did not believe that I had GBS but rather TM. Surprisingly to all of us in the room, he also made some disparaging remarks about the staff neurologist and called for a repeat of the EMG/NCS tests. His brusque manner and disrespect for his medical colleague struck us all as quite unprofessional. Combined with the low quality of care I was receiving, my friends had already begun a plan to remove me from the South Bend hospital in favor of taking me to the Mayo Clinic in Rochester, MN, a world-renowned medical center in my own home state. In the light of that plan, Perry had gone to my residence at Notre Dame to pack up my belongings for the trip to Minnesota.

In response to the chief neurologist's statements, George informed him of the plan, exclaiming: "That's it! We want out." The chief neurologist replied that he was the doctor and he would decide when I could leave. George reminded him that patients have rights and one of those rights was to change doctors and hospitals. He again asked the chief neurologist to arrange to have me transferred to Mayo. The chief neurologist said that Mayo wouldn't accept me as a patient because the officials at Mayo were his friends and he would not recommend my transfer. He then walked out, effectively ending the conversation.

In fact, Mayo had already tentatively accepted me for admission as a result of discussions my friends had with officials at St. Mary's Hospital earlier in the day. St. Mary's is part of the Mayo Clinic, with a long history of cooperation with the Franciscan Sisters based in Rochester, MN. (I had developed a lengthy and mutually supportive relationship with the sisters there since I had frequently sent them manuscripts of my church compositions for their use, led enrichment programs for students at St. Theresa's College in Winona, MN [a Catholic institution of higher learning sponsored by the Rochester Franciscans], and had celebrated Masses at the Franciscan motherhouse at Assisi Heights. I think Kevin's influence as an important figure in the Archdiocese's governance and as someone who had made significant contacts with many Catholic institutions in the United States was important in getting me admitted, but I also believe that my previous relationship with the Rochester Franciscans may have influenced the decision to admit me.)

Kevin had earlier called a contact he had at Notre Dame to see if the university would be willing to transport me to Mayo Clinic by means of their jet. The official said that normally they would be willing to do so, but that the jet was presently in South America on a scouting trip to interview some possible student-athletes. He and Tom then began to explore other ways of getting me to Mayo from South Bend, eventually settling on a group called Air Angels, Inc., a corporation providing emergency medical transport by helicopter.

The focus of attention now shifted to the practicalities of leaving the South Bend hospital. George and Perry decided to drive at about 9:30 PM back to the Twin Cities to check on my house there, followed by a journey to Rochester, to help me adjust to the new hospital setting. George told Kevin and Tom to make sure that I was in Rochester the next day when he would meet me there. Vicki, Tom, and Kevin made a plan to get my car out of the hospital parking lot and to drive it back to the Twin Cities the following day. I prepared myself for my first helicopter ride.

23 April 2003   *Easter Wednesday*

The Air Angel pilots and attendant arrived at the South Bend hospital the next morning. They prepared me for the flight by strapping me to a stretcher and completely enshrouding me with restrictive clothes so that I would not shift position during the flight. Just before they took me to the helicopter, Vicki, Tom, and Kevin said *bon voyage* and wished me a good flight, assuring me that they'd see me in Rochester. Always helpful and attentive to details others might miss, Vicki took my watch since it was clear that I wouldn't be needing it for a while.

On a lighter note, I'm happy to report that Kevin and Tom, along with Vicki, decided to spend a little time having fun on the drive back home since the original plan had been to take a mini-vacation when they visited me. They stopped off at a casino in Wisconsin Dells, WI, stayed overnight, and returned to the Twin Cities the next day.

While I didn't mind being enshrouded for the trip, I did feel somewhat cheated that, given where Air Angel personnel positioned the stretcher, I couldn't see out of the helicopter to observe the journey. The distance from the South Bend hospital to the Mayo Clinic was so great that we had to land about midway through the trip for refueling. George was there to welcome me soon after we landed at the heliport on the roof of St. Mary's Hospital in Rochester.

The contrast between my treatment at the South Bend hospital and the Mayo Clinic could not have been greater. No definitive diagnosis had been determined in the three days I had spent at the South Bend hospital. Immediately upon exiting the helicopter at St. Mary's Hospital, multiple personnel swarmed around me, placing my stretcher on a gurney, positioning a blood pressure cuff on my right arm, and swiftly getting me inside the hospital. A resident by the name of Dr. Dove was leading the team that brought me into St. Mary's. After about twenty minutes of testing and having read the chart information that traveled with me from South Bend, Dr. Dove told me: "We have to wait for my supervising physician to confirm this, but I am 95% sure that you have Guillain-Barré. I can tell you that you will get better. But you will probably get much worse before you do."

As I recall it, a profound sense of relief rushed through me at Dr. Dove's words. After all the confusion, I had finally received a diagnosis. Hearing his medical verdict dispelled the chaos and confusion I had been feeling. Even if my future involved suffering as the syndrome ran its course, at least I would have a sense of what was happening to me and could make tentative plans about my return to health.

This is the last vivid memory I have until I came to consciousness once again in about two weeks. I will try to describe my experiences in the neurological intensive care unit and the ventilator unit at St. Mary's in chapter three.

REFLECTIONS

What did my experience of waiting for a diagnosis teach me?

First, I became aware of how privileged I was in terms of social status, class, and economic resources. I hold a doctorate and am usually quite skilled in communication, yet I found myself confused and unsure about what medical personnel told me once I entered the hospital. I was no longer an expert, or more accurately, the knowledge that gave me a certain social status as a priest and professor was not particularly valued or helpful in the new social status I occupied as a patient. I had medical insurance as an employee of the Archdiocese of St. Paul and Minneapolis, so there was no difficulty in admitting me to the hospital. To this day I wonder if I had not been a priest-professor whether or not the Air Angels would have agreed to transport me to Rochester. My friends could attest to my social status and my ability to pay for the services rendered, but what if I were alone and confused and trying to decide my future on my own? In fact, I later learned that my entire experience with GBS cost the Archdiocese of St. Paul and Minneapolis' insurance company approximately $500,000, so that the $50,000 it cost for air transport to Mayo Clinic seems almost paltry in comparison. Being a priest meant that I belonged to a network of relationships in various Catholic institutions, a network that was disposed to treat me well. Even the move from my initial room to the VIP suite at the South Bend hospital seems to be both an apology for my earlier treatment and a recognition of my social status.

Second, it made me incredibly grateful for my family and friends. In the light of what I experienced later as my GBS progressed, I think it likely that I could have died or been left with significant neurological impairment if I had stayed at the South Bend hospital. The experience of leaving the South Bend hospital and being admitted to the Mayo Clinic made me aware of just how important it is to have advocates who will plead your case to those charged with your medical care. I could only imagine what it would be like for someone who did not speak English or one of the "recognized" alternative languages (e.g., Spanish for much of the United States, Hmong and Somali for the Twin Cities) to communicate with the already busy hospital personnel.

Third, I understood why having an accurate diagnosis is so important in the life of a patient. Without an agreed-upon diagnosis, one's treatment is at best palliative, not oriented toward cure. But once a diagnosis is settled upon, plans can be made toward reversing the progress of the ailment one is suffering. I think this is a principle that applies not only to physical suffering but to psychological and spiritual suffering as well. As long as there is no diagnosis, one's neuroses or psychoses can remain in power, but by identifying the ailment (e.g., an addiction to alcohol) a variety of paths to wellness (e.g., a Twelve-Step program with abstinence from consciousness-altering substances) can be chosen. As long as there is no diagnosis, a deep resentment toward God (e.g., arising from the death of a loved one) can poison one's prayer, but naming such a state of soul allows grace to enter and transform one's perspective and soul. In any case I was grateful that I had finally been diagnosed so that I could begin the process of healing under the guidance of the medical personnel at Mayo.

Suggested listening

I confess to a real affection for the composition I've chosen to represent the time of diagnosis. The text of "A Shelter in the Time of Storm" was written by Vernon John Charlesworth ca. 1880. When Ira David Sankey composed his hymn tune SHELTER (LM with Refrain) for this text in 1885, he slightly adapted the text. I, in turn, further adapted the text and emphasized the "call/response" pattern of the verses in order to create a contemporary spiritual.

I associate "A Shelter in the Time of Storm" with the stage of diagnosis in my battle with GBS. Just as the psalms laud God as "rock of refuge," "shield and fortress," "rescuing hand" and "protector," having a trustworthy diagnosis allows one afflicted to find a "refuge in the weary land" of suffering. I deliberately set the text for an *a cappella* choir because, to my ear, voices without any instrumental accompaniment sound quite vulnerable and seem to connect with listeners with real intensity. I chose the musical idiom of the black spiritual because our African-American brothers and sisters created such powerful expressions of trust in God through suffering by means of Gospel songs and spirituals. I hope listeners will consider this a genuine homage to this heritage on my part and not judge it another example of a white person stealing from black artistic responses to suffering.

1. The Lord's a rock and in him we hide:
   A shelter in the time of storm.
   He bids us come and with him abide:
   A shelter in the time of storm.

   O my Jesus is a refuge in a weary land,
   a weary land, a weary land.
   O my Jesus is a refuge in a weary land,
   a refuge in the time of storm.

2. A shade by day, a defense by night:
   A shelter in the time of storm.
   No fears alarm and no foes affright:
   A shelter in the time of storm.

   O my Jesus is a refuge in a weary land,
   a weary land, a weary land.
   O my Jesus is a refuge in a weary land,
   a shelter in the time of storm.

3. The raging storms may around us beat:
   A shelter in the time of storm.
   We'll never leave our safe retreat:
   A shelter in the time of storm.

   O my Jesus is a refuge in a weary land,
   a weary land, a weary land.
   O my Jesus is a refuge in a weary land,
   a shelter in a time of storm.

4. O rock divine and a refuge dear:
   A shelter in the time of storm.
   Come be our helper who's ever near:
   A shelter in the time of storm.

   O my Jesus is a refuge in a weary land,
   a weary land, a weary land.
   O my Jesus is a refuge in a weary land,
   a shelter in the time of storm.

"A Shelter in the Time of Storm" appears on the Oregon Catholic Press CD-20612 O God of Past and Present. Copies of the CD and sheet music can be purchased from the Oregon Catholic Press website (www.ocp.org) or at Oregon Catholic Press, 5536 N.E. Hassalo, Portland, OR 97213.

A recorded version of the composition may be accessed at **www.youtube.com/watch?v=901JKPQ9OEw**

Interlude

GUILLAIN-BARRÉ SYNDROME

Now that we have reached a point in my narrative where I have received a confirmed diagnosis of GBS, I think readers may want to know about this condition in some detail. Fortunately, the **National Institute of Neurological Disorders and Stroke** *(a division of the National Institutes of Health) has prepared an excellent fact sheet on GBS that may be freely copied. As will become clear in the rest of this memoir, I presented almost a textbook case of this malady.*

What is
Guillain-Barré syndrome?

Guillain-Barré syndrome (GBS) is a disorder in which the body's immune system attacks part of the peripheral nervous system. The first symptoms of this disorder include varying degrees of weakness or tingling sensations in the legs. In many instances the symmetrical weakness and abnormal sensations spread to the arms and upper body. These symptoms can increase in intensity until certain muscles cannot be used at all and, when severe, the person is almost totally paralyzed. In these cases the disorder is life threatening—potentially interfering with breathing and, at times, with blood pressure or heart rate—and is considered a medical emergency. Such an individual is often put on a ventilator to assist with breathing and is watched closely for problems such as an abnormal heart beat, infections, blood clots, and high or low blood pressure. Most individuals, however, have good recovery from even the most severe cases of Guillain-Barré syndrome, although some continue to have a certain degree of weakness.

Guillain-Barré syndrome can affect anybody. It can strike at any age and both sexes are equally prone to the disorder. The syndrome is rare, however, afflicting only about one person in 100,000. Usually Guillain-Barré occurs a few days or weeks after the patient has had symptoms of a respiratory or gastrointestinal viral infection. Occasionally surgery will trigger the syndrome. Recently, some countries worldwide have reported an increased incidence of GBS following infection with the Zika virus. In rare instances vaccinations may increase the risk of GBS.

After the first clinical manifestations of the disease, the symptoms can progress over the course of hours, days, or weeks. Most people reach the stage of greatest weakness within the first two weeks after symptoms appear, and by the third week of the illness ninety percent of all patients are at their weakest.

....

What causes
Guillain-Barré syndrome?

No one yet knows why Guillain-Barré—which is not contagious—strikes some people and not others. Nor does anyone know exactly what sets the disease in motion.

What scientists do know is that the body's immune system begins to attack the body itself, causing what is known as an autoimmune disease. Usually the cells of the immune system attack only foreign material and invading organisms. In Guillain-Barré syndrome, however, the immune system starts to destroy the myelin sheath that surrounds the axons of many peripheral nerves, or even the axons themselves (axons are long, thin extensions of the nerve cells; they carry nerve signals). The myelin sheath surrounding the axon speeds up the transmission of nerve signals and allows the transmission of signals over long distances.

In diseases in which the peripheral nerves' myelin sheaths are injured or degraded, the nerves cannot transmit signals efficiently. That is why the muscles begin to lose their ability to respond to the brain's commands, commands that must be carried through the nerve network. The brain also receives fewer sensory signals from the rest of the body, resulting in an inability to feel textures, heat, pain, and other sensations. Alternately, the brain may receive inappropriate signals that result in tingling, "crawling-skin," or painful sensations. Because the signals to and from the arms and legs must travel the longest distances they are most vulnerable to interruption. Therefore, muscle weakness and tingling sensations usually first appear in the hands and feet and progress upwards.

When Guillain-Barré is preceded by a viral or bacterial infection, it is possible that the virus has changed the nature of cells in the nervous system so that the immune system treats them as foreign cells. It is also possible that the virus makes the immune system itself less discriminating about what cells it recognizes as its own, allowing some of the immune cells, such as certain kinds of lymphocytes and macrophages, to attack the myelin. Sensitized T lymphocytes cooperate with B lymphocytes to produce antibodies against components of the myelin sheath and may contribute to destruction of the myelin. In two forms of GBS, axons are attacked by antibodies against the bacteria Campylobacter jejuni, which react with proteins of the peripheral nerves. Acute motor axonal neuropathy is particularly common in Chinese children. Scientists are investigating these and other possibilities to find why the immune system goes awry in Guillain-Barré syndrome and other autoimmune diseases. The cause and course of Guillain-Barré syndrome is an active area of neurological investigation, incorporating the cooperative efforts of neurological scientists, immunologists, and virologists.

....

How is Guillain-Barré syndrome diagnosed?

Guillain-Barré is called a syndrome rather than a disease because it is not clear that a specific disease-causing agent is involved. A syndrome is a medical condition characterized by a collection of symptoms (what the patient feels) and signs (what a doctor can observe or measure). The signs and symptoms of the syndrome can be quite varied, so doctors may, on rare occasions, find it difficult to diagnose Guillain-Barré in its earliest stages.

Several disorders have symptoms similar to those found in Guillain-Barré, so doctors examine and question patients carefully before making a diagnosis. Collectively, the signs and symptoms form a certain pattern that helps doctors differentiate Guillain-Barré from other disorders. For example, physicians will note whether the symptoms appear on both sides of the body (most common in Guillain-Barré) and the quickness with which the symptoms appear (in other disorders, muscle weakness may progress over months rather than days or weeks). In Guillain-Barré, reflexes such as knee jerks are usually lost. Because the signals traveling along the nerve are slower, a nerve conduction velocity (NCV) test can give a doctor clues to aid the diagnosis. In Guillain-Barré patients, the cerebrospinal fluid that bathes the spinal cord and brain contains more protein than usual. Therefore a physician may decide to perform a spinal tap, a procedure in which a needle is inserted into the patient's lower back and a small amount of cerebrospinal fluid from the spinal column is withdrawn for study.

....

How is Guillain-Barré treated?

There is no known cure for Guillain-Barré syndrome. However, there are therapies that lessen the severity of the illness and accelerate the recovery in most patients. There are also a number of ways to treat the complications of the disease.

Currently, plasma exchange (also called plasmapheresis) and high-dose immunoglobulin therapy are used. Both of them are equally effective, but immunoglobulin is easier to administer. Plasma exchange is a method by which whole blood is removed from the body and processed so that the red and white blood cells are separated from the plasma, or liquid portion of the blood. The blood cells are then returned to the patient without the plasma, which the body quickly replaces. Scientists still don't know exactly why plasma exchange works, but the technique seems to reduce the severity and duration of the Guillain-Barré episode. This may be because plasmapheresis can remove antibodies and other immune cell-derived factors that could contribute to nerve damage.

In high-dose immunoglobulin therapy, doctors give intravenous injections of the proteins that, in small quantities, the immune system uses naturally to attack invading organisms. Investigators have found that giving high doses of these immunoglobulins, derived from a pool of thousands of normal donors, to Guillain-Barré patients can lessen the immune attack on the nervous system. Investigators don't know why or how this works, although several hypotheses have been proposed.

The use of steroid hormones has also been tried as a way to reduce the severity of Guillain-Barré, but controlled clinical trials have demonstrated that this treatment not only is not effective but may even have a deleterious effect on the disease.

The most critical part of the treatment for this syndrome consists of keeping the patient's body functioning during recovery of the nervous system. This can sometimes require placing the patient on mechanical ventilatory assistance, a heart monitor, or other machines that assist body function. The need for this sophisticated machinery is one reason why Guillain-Barré syndrome patients are usually treated in hospitals, often in an intensive care ward. In the hospital, doctors can also look for and treat the many problems that can afflict any paralyzed patient—complications such as pneumonia or bed sores.

Often, even before recovery begins, caregivers may be instructed to manually move the patient's limbs to help keep the muscles flexible and strong and to prevent venous sludging (the buildup of red blood cells in veins, which could lead to reduced blood flow) in the limbs which could result in deep vein thrombosis. Later, as the patient begins to recover limb control, physical therapy begins. Carefully planned clinical trials of new and experimental therapies are the key to improving the treatment of patients with Guillain-Barré syndrome. Such clinical trials begin with the research of basic and clinical scientists who, working with clinicians, identify new approaches to treating patients with the disease.

What is the long-term outlook for those with Guillain-Barré syndrome?

Guillain-Barré syndrome can be a devastating disorder because of its sudden and unexpected onset. In addition, recovery is not necessarily quick. As noted above, patients usually reach the point of greatest weakness or paralysis days or weeks after the first symptoms occur. Symptoms then stabilize at this level for a period of days, weeks, or, sometimes, months. The recovery period may be as little as a few weeks or as long as a few years. About thirty percent of those with Guillain-Barré still have a residual weakness after three years. About 3 percent may suffer a relapse of muscle weakness and tingling sensations many years after the initial attack.

Guillain-Barré syndrome patients face not only physical difficulties, but emotionally painful periods as well. It is often extremely difficult for patients to adjust to sudden paralysis and dependence on others for help with routine daily activities. Patients sometimes need psychological counseling to help them adapt.

From: "Guillain-Barré Syndrome Fact Sheet," **National Institute of Neurological Disorders and Stroke Publication,** *National Institutes of Health Publication No. 11-2902 (July 2011)*

*It may be helpful for readers to know that GBS is known
under a variety of names: Acute inflammatory demyelinating
polyneuropathy (AIDP), Landry's ascending paralysis, or French
polio. There are a variety of clinical subtypes of the syndrome as
well as a chronic form (CIDP) that affects only approximately 5%
of those with the syndrome.*

*For those who might want further information about GBS
and related autoimmune maladies, the GBS/ICDP Foundation
International publishes a periodical called* **The Communicator**.
*This periodical publishes patients' stories, summaries of cutting-
edge research, honors received by various members of the GBS
community, and suggestions for how to get involved in supporting
and advocating for those who come down with these illnesses.
Write to* **375 E. Elm Street, Suite 101 / Conshohocken, PA 19428**
to subscribe.

CHAPTER THREE

The Abyss

THE STORY

23 April 2003   *Easter Wednesday*

I arrived by helicopter on the roof of St. Mary's Hospital about 4 PM on Easter Wednesday. George, my mother, and my sister Stacie were all at the hospital to welcome me to "Domitilla 2," a particular ward in the hospital. According to their memories, I was surrounded by five or six Air Angels in blue or black flight suits.

Stacie noticed that I was all tucked up under a white blanket with black seatbelts crossing my chest and with only my head peeking out. As I was wheeled into my room, Stacie said: "You are all tucked in like a little papoose," to which the flight people replied: "Do you know this person?" ☺

Stacie stayed in my room that first night at Mayo. Fortunately she had brought a sleeping bag that was functional down to zero degrees Fahrenheit, because my room was set at 56 degrees Fahrenheit. My body was very warm, a characteristic of GBS, where both body temperature and blood pressure can fluctuate wildly, so the room temperature was set to make me more comfortable. I was given special socks to wear that would squeeze my legs at various points to keep from developing blood clots. Because my hands could no longer hold things very well, I was concerned about being able to call the nurse. I received a very sensitive nurse call button that was placed under my hand where the slightest pressure would set it off. Unfortunately it just kept going off, seemingly on its own, so eventually the nurse told me simply to let Stacie know if I needed anything.

It was a difficult and restless night because I couldn't find a position in which I felt comfortable. (Another characteristic of GBS is difficulty in interpreting what the nerves associated with posture were communicating.) Finally, Stacie rolled me over on my side and held me there which seemed to work rather well.

24 April 2003   *Easter Thursday*

As Thursday dawned I was having more and more difficulty

breathing. The blood gas and oxygen monitor showed that I wasn't getting enough oxygen as the peripheral nerves controlling my respiration began to fail. The decision was made to move me to the neurological intensive care unit (ICU) where it would be easier to place me on a ventilator if that became necessary. This was a wise decision because almost immediately upon getting to the ICU my blood pressure began to fluctuate and my breathing became more labored. I was intubated as a precaution in case my breathing failed, and that made it difficult to communicate (I couldn't speak with a tube in my throat).

Sometime during the day I had my first IVIg treatment. Although I had been treated with steroids at the South Bend hospital, my Mayo doctors recognized that such treatment was not called for once I had been diagnosed with GBS. (I also learned that the treatment I was eventually given could not be introduced until the steroids had left my system.) I later learned that there are two courses of action that were recommended to try and "jump start" the peripheral nerves whose myelin sheath insulation was being steadily stripped away by my immune system. One, called "plasmapheresis," involves separating and removing the plasma from the blood to remove whatever diseased substance may be circulating in the plasma. After the plasma is removed, the patient's red and white blood cells and platelets, along with a replacement fluid, are reintroduced into the patient's blood stream. One could think of this as blood cleansing, insofar as it attempts to remove aberrant protein from the plasma and replace it with donor plasma or a plasma substitute. The other, intravenous immunoglobulin therapy (IVIg), gives the patient antibodies that the body is not making on its own to prevent infections. Liquid immunoglobulin is taken from the blood plasma of healthy donors, collected and purified, and then flows from a bag through a needle into the patient's vein, a procedure that takes two to four hours. Studies on these courses of action revealed them to be about equally effective, so the decision was made to go with a round of IVIg infusions.

Kevin, Tom, and Vicki stopped by at about 5 PM, but I was sleeping, so I didn't know they were there until later in the evening. Thursday night was again not very restful since my back hurt, my body temperature was very warm, and my blood pressure kept swinging from low to high and back without any predictability. I remember using my energy to try to communicate how grateful I was to everyone who had watched over me to this point and that I loved them. Since I am deeply introverted by nature I'm not particularly emotionally demonstrative and would rarely tell family and friends that I loved them, so those who had gathered interpreted my messages as though I had begun to lose hope and that I feared I was going to die. In fact, I don't remember having that fear, but I couldn't communicate that to my family and friends, and they grew quite sad.

Stacie once again took the night shift and tried to make me as comfortable as possible while I continued to experience the restlessness and pain that I had the night before. During the night in addition to the "squeezing socks," my feet were slipped into sheepskin boots to keep them upright, i.e., to avoid a future case of "drop foot," an abnormality in walking stemming from difficulty in lifting the front part of the foot.

25 April 2003   Easter Friday

Because I was in such discomfort and exhibited much agitation, the medical personnel decided to treat me with "propofol," a medication that instigates a decreased level of consciousness (sedation) and a lack of memory for events (amnesiac). This medication was remarkably effective in my case because I have no memory of what I went through for the next week and a half or so. Thus the details I will share of my experiences in the ICU rely on the journals kept by my family and friends during the ordeal. It is quite disconcerting to discover from their writings that I acted as though I were wide awake and conscious of events at the time, while I have no memory of these events at all. I was also given morphine for the pain I was experiencing and to calm the thrashing I continued to do. I also received a second IVIg treatment.

I would like to share two dreams and an incident I remember from this period, giving the reader a sense of how my consciousness reacted to the medications I received.

In the first vivid dream I was an actor playing a detec-

tive in a Canadian-based television series. The female lead
was played by Joni Mitchell, and the two of us, based in
Montreal and speaking both French and English, would
follow cases to Toronto, Winnipeg, Edmonton, Banf, and
Vancouver, with a different cast of characters in each city.
(I realized later that the pattern was lifted from *Route 66*, a
TV show I had watched with great interest in my youth.)
The major conflict was behind the scenes in which other
cast members and crew objected to my leading man role
in the series, since I was a United States citizen. It all culmi-
nated in an episode in which we came to the Mayo Clinic
in Rochester, MN, to investigate the CEO for malfeasance,
breaking into his very modern office on the ninth floor of
St. Mary's Hospital.

The second vivid dream was even more strange. Dressed
in sackcloth, I was lying on a litter before the altar of what
appeared to be a small medieval parish church with wattled
walls and thatched roof. I knew I was the pastor of this small
community and that I was lying paralyzed before the altar
attempting to plead with God for the good of my parish-
ioners. I noticed that the setting was truly medieval insofar as there were sheep and goats wandering in the aisles
of the church. After what seemed like hours, members of
the neighboring monastery came to bring me in procession to the monastery church. This single monastery had
both male and female members and I was entranced by the
harmonies they sang on the road. We reached the monastery just as the Vespers bells were ringing at sunset. The

monks and nuns laid me down in the middle of the Lady chapel of their monastic church and began to sing Vespers (Evening Prayer). As they were singing, all of the monks and nuns began to glow from within and were transformed into living stained glass, tilting back and extending their hands as they sang in the light of the setting sun. Later on I felt like the composer Robert Schumann, hallucinating the glorious singing of angels but unable to notate it before they fell to silence. I still think this might have been the most beautiful music I have ever heard.

A third instance from this period that walks the border-line between reality and fantasy arises from a long evening in which I tried to inform my male nurse attendant that the head of the department was a criminal whom I had shot and killed the previous day. I remember him actually coming to my bedside while I tried to explain to him why he needed to go to the head of the department's office to confirm the death. Looking back on the experience, I'm sure I was totally incoherent and puzzling to the nurse attendant since I was intubated and on a ventilator and thus unable to talk, but I have a rather vivid memory of him trying to decipher what I was saying. I also remember wondering whether or not I had in fact murdered the head of the department, posing the question of how I could ascertain that fact if I could only think about it rather than have any concrete evidence that the event had actually occurred.

26 April 2003   *Easter Saturday*

I had my third IVIg treatment as the doctors charged with my care told George, Vicki, and my family members that I had hit bottom, with recovery taking weeks, not days. My paralysis had reached the stage where I could only voluntarily blink one eye, but that was still better than either death or "locked-in syndrome," a terrifying-to-me situation in which your brain is clear and working so as to hear what's going on but the paralysis is so complete that there is no way to communicate with the outside world; while rare, both of these conditions can result from GBS. George and Vicki taught me how to communicate by "blink-spelling." As they signaled the beginning of the process I was to blink once for the first half of the alphabet or twice for the second half. They would then recite the letters in order and I was to blink when they hit the proper letter.

Rather quickly, the flaws in this system were revealed. As a former English major, I pride myself on my concern for proper grammar. Thus I began by blink-spelling out complete sentences, although we had no signal for the conclusion of one word and the beginning of another. This led to a frequently repeated chant from those trying to decipher what I was communicating: "Just one word at a time, NOT a whole sentence." Then I sometimes blink-spelled the wrong word to the great confusion of my interlocutors. For example, I took to calling my hospital gown a "jacket" and asked that it be taken off or readjusted when

I was feeling particularly hot. George and Vicki were completely confused by my reference to a jacket, and it took some time to figure out that I meant my hospital gown. Of course, during that time I grew increasingly impatient and frustrated. (Eventually, we could laugh about this and similar incidents.)

One of the disadvantages of being completely paralyzed except for one eye is that the facial muscles cannot communicate one's emotional state accurately. I have to say that I don't remember ever wanting to die throughout this entire ordeal when I was "awake." I do remember wanting the pain to stop, but that didn't mean I wanted my caretakers to "pull the plug." Even though I don't remember judging that I was dying and wanting my caretakers to just turn off the ventilator, Vicki, George and some of my family members interpreted the look on my face that way. George took up the responsibility of reassuring me that I would get better, even if it didn't seem that I was making any progress whatsoever.

---

27 April 2003   *Sunday*

I had my fourth IVIg treatment on the Second Sunday of Easter. I sensed that the doctors were getting somewhat nervous in that I didn't seem to be responding to this therapeutic intervention.

I was fairly miserable because it was so hard to communicate; apparently I was trying to blink-spell something that began with "p" and no one was able to decipher it. My blood pressure was quite high and I continued thrashing around, so they decided to sedate me.

A changing of the guard took place among my family and friends: Vicki arrived about noon; my sister Kathy arrived for her overnight shift about 1 AM, so my mother and Stacie could go back home.

28 April 2003   Monday

About 1:30 PM the nurses bathed and shaved me, the concluding actions begun with washing my hair earlier in the weekend. Although I had my fifth IVIg treatment on this day, I continued to thrash around with high blood pressure. By 3:30 PM both my blood pressure and my breathing on the ventilator stabilized and the doctor opined that from now on it was simply a waiting game to see when the myelin sheaths surrounding my peripheral nerves would reconstitute themselves so that I would be able to move again. George continued to assure me that he wouldn't put me through this if he didn't feel I'd eventually be OK.

A bright spot marking Monday was that my visitors were allowed to oversee my sucking on lemon-flavored swabs to assuage my intense thirst. They were cautioned to be very careful since my swallowing reflex had not come back in any detectable way.

My cousin Margaret, a doctor-anesthesiologist employed by Mayo Clinic, came to visit, but I wasn't really awake to interact with her. Patrice came to stay overnight that day and the next, returning with my mother. Overnight I had the mucus in my ventilator tube suctioned out twice by one of the nurses.

29 April 2003   *Tuesday*

My overnight experience was unremarkable except for a new treatment. Just as the staff had employed an airflow blanket to cool me down when feverish, now they employed another aspect of my bed's capabilities which was to pummel my back to loosen any lung congestion. By all reports I enjoyed the process, possibly because it kept me from simply lying in the same position for hours on end.

At his 10 AM visit my case doctor said that I could be miserable for another week or two as the syndrome took its course. He let us know that he was debating whether or not to try plasmapheresis since the IVIg treatments didn't seem to be working.

In the afternoon I developed yet another fever and George and Vicki wet washcloths in ice water to pat down my body. The nurses were in awe of Vicki's ability to lower my blood pressure by her presence and cold-cloth technique. Eventually a nurse covered me with an air-flow blanket that let me sleep about four hours. I was also prescribed haloperidol for anxiety and put on a new antibiotic, metronidazole, used to treat bacterial infections of the stomach and respiratory tract, as well as other uses. In addition to these drugs, I continued to take cephalexin (another antibiotic), propofol (to keep me relaxed because of my intubation), and fentanyl (a synthetic opioid pain medication). We were all in awe of the medical community's ability to prescribe and monitor these drugs for harmful interactions.

---

30 April 2003   *Wednesday*

At around 5:45 AM, Patrice and my mother observed that I was able to shrug my shoulders and answer "yes" and "no" questions with the appropriate head shake, all signs that some muscle control was returning. By 7:25 AM my blood pressure and heart rhythm were both normal and things appeared to be improving. Perhaps most important, I was taken off propofol and began the process of remembering my coming to consciousness (i.e., "waking up"). The chief neurologist on the floor ordered another suctioning of my ventilator tube and lungs (a "snot suck") to guarantee that there was no fluid buildup, but in fact I had developed pneumonia so had to be treated with new antibiotics.

By 11:50 AM my blood pressure shifted to borderline low, but it recovered after I was moved around a bit. The staff assured those watching over me that this rapid alternation of low and high blood pressure (like the rapid alternation of body temperature) is a normal sign of GBS, but a dangerous one that needed to be monitored carefully.

A nurse told George that now was the worst time of my life, but I would get better. I suspected in response to her faith in my recovery, George and Vicki met with a social worker to start making plans for rehab once I graduated from the ICU and could breathe on my own. The leading candidates: either rehabilitation at Mayo, a rehabilitation hospital such as the Sister Kenny Institute associated with Abbot-Northwestern Hospital in Minneapolis, Bethesda Rehabilitation Hospital in St. Paul, or one of about eighty nursing homes in the Twin Cities area.

I didn't realize it at the time, but Ed and Ginny Bartch, two members of Eau Claire Newman, George's parish, were at the Mayo Clinic at the same time I was to attend to Ed's health issues. They took George out for a good meal that evening, the same evening that two friends from Minneapolis, John Estrem and Joan Gecik, arrived to take Vicki out for a similar repast. I am so grateful to them because it became clear to me later on that my caretakers needed respite from the tension involved in witnessing my fragile progress. All later joined my mother and sister Stacie for a discussion of my future. Meanwhile I had once again stabilized and when they all came to say good night I was fast asleep without the air-flow blanket.

1 May 2003	*Thursday*

This day marked two weeks since noticing some muscle weakness while celebrating the Holy Thursday liturgy.

My morning was marked by extremity checks, which confirmed that there were some small signs of improvement: I could move my fingers a little and I was moving some muscles in my thighs and upper shoulders. I do have a vivid memory of being able to move the fourth finger on my right hand and being flooded with a sense of joy I had not had in years. The only frustrating part was that I grew tired very quickly and could not sustain these motions consistently for any length of time.

I underwent tracheostomy surgery around midday, a procedure by which a tube was inserted into my windpipe to open my restricted airway and enable breathing. I later learned that this procedure is sometimes called a stoma, which more properly refers to the hole in my neck (Greek *stoma* = mouth) through which the tube is inserted. In some ways I thought I had hit rock bottom by undergoing the procedure. Mere intubation signaled to me that my caretakers thought I'd be making a recovery fairly soon, but having a tube quasi-permanently inserted through my neck suggested that the muscles controlling my respiration might take a long time to fire up again, if ever.

My friends started a CaringBridge website for me. (For readers who may not know, CaringBridge is a 501 (c)(3) nonprofit organization that runs a website by which people can easily get updates on a person's condition and offer support and encouragement.) They had earlier decided that they needed to limit those who had physical contact with me, since I mostly needed rest and a sterile environment. CaringBridge became the perfect way to inform people of my progress while at the same time shielding me from people who might sap the energy I needed for healing.

That evening my fever returned, but by now the responses to it were becoming standard: my nurse gave me ibuprofen, Vicki and my sister Kathy, who were taking the overnight shift, patted me down with cool wet washcloths, and the air-flow blanket was restored.

2 May 2003   *Friday*

My CaringBridge website had received more than two thousand hits in the short time that it had been up. Vicki kept track of the emails and cards and reported that many of the messages were quite touching.

George, Vicki, and Kim took turns swabbing my lips so that I could get some hydration. They graduated from the lemon swabs I mentioned earlier to pink swabs that could be dipped in a variety of liquids. Water, decaffeinated Diet Coke, and regular Diet Coke seemed to be my liquids of choice. There was some debate about whether or not I should be having this hydration since the wound around the stoma of my tracheostomy had not completely healed and there was still some debate about my swallow reflex. What was not debatable was how absolutely delicious these liquids tasted!

My sister Kim came for her overnight shift. About 1 AM, when she visited my room, she first saw the nurses suctioning out my tracheostomy, apparently removing a sizeable amount of mucus. As Kim reported: "Very good that you were getting the stuff out but made me feel a little dizzy-woozy—had to sit down. So much for my medical career!"

Just as my family had worked out a pattern of visitation where my mother stayed rather consistently at the hospital but individual sisters and brothers came for overnight shifts, so George and Vicki worked out a pattern where George would return to his parish for his weekend responsibilities, returning Sunday afternoon or Monday morning and staying until Friday or Saturday, Vicki would stay over the weekend and return to her job during the week, returning on Thursday or Friday.

(One of the most encouraging things about my family and friends is that they all have quirky senses of humor. For example, Vicki couldn't stop laughing when George reported to her about my "bugle numbers" [a measure of my lungs' ability to expel air], since she thought the term was so odd. When I developed a low-grade fever later in the day she informed me that this might be the first time I had ever had a low grade. I came to appreciate how much humor has to do with healing.)

I remember asking my sister Kim if there was any hope that I would walk again and she said that the indications were absolutely "yes"—that I would probably fully recover. I found that as I "woke up" more and more from my previous sedation that I needed reassurances from many of my visitors that I was making progress and would return to health. Of course, I knew that none of us could predict the future, but just hearing their confident responses was heartening.

Apparently I tried to communicate that I had had the dream I mentioned above about Joni Mitchell, but my blink-spelling skills as well as Vicki's interpretative ones were not up to the effort. When I inquired about where George was, Vicki reminded me that he had gone home to his parish for the weekend but would be back on Monday.

All of my caretakers noticed that my eyes never completely closed even when it was clear that I was unconscious and asleep. Eventually the nurses added some ointment to my eyelids so that my eyes would not dry out during my sleep periods.

4 May 2003   *Sunday*

This was a relatively quiet day except for some leg stretching guided by a physical therapist. Both Vicki and my family members felt that I was much more animated than they had seen me, asking for my glasses (but definitely NOT to watch television). Most of our conversation consisted of stories, including one Vicki had found on the CaringBridge website from a man named Glenn Miller (!) who had had GBS and was jogging six months later. (I confess to a rather nasty, inappropriate response when she told me the story: "O goody-goody gumdrops for him!" ☺)

George arrived about 3:30 PM and Kathy arrived around 7 PM for her overnight shift, along with her daughter/my niece Lauren. What should have been a restful night after the advances of the weekend brought a real scare. About

11:15 PM an alarm went off in my room, both waking me from sleep and indicating that I couldn't breathe. This was really the first time I remember having to have my ventilator tube and bronchia suctioned out. The hospital personnel detached the tube and removed a great plug of mucus, but since I couldn't breathe while they were doing their work, I was terrified, sure that I would suffocate to death. I called for George in case he'd have to pray the prayers commending the dying. After that experience I wasn't able to sleep for the rest of the night.

In retrospect I realized that the tube had been detached at the most for a minute and I certainly wouldn't die in that amount of time. Eventually being "bronched" became routine.

5 May 2003   *Monday*

Vicki arrived at 7:30 AM to be greeted by the story of the nighttime scare. She and George attempted to keep me awake through the day so that I could sleep through the night. The physical therapist who had seen me last Friday declared that she could detect real improvement in my ability to stretch and my movements. The high point of the day occurred when I was given cranberry juice on a swab.

About 5:45 PM my brother Joe and my mother arrived for their overnight watch. I think the reader will get a hint of the kind of humor that marks our family communication from Joe's entry in the night journal that the family kept: "Ed (the night nurse) let me watch your assessment. He gave you lots of meds and potassium and a blood thinner. He suctioned your tube. He suctioned your mouth. I told Ed that I had the talent and you got the chicks!" In an attempt to support my overnight sleep, the nurses began to enforce a rule that I was to have no visitors from 12 midnight until 6 AM. Joe's comment: "So I went to the family room and watched the Wild game (which they won!)."

---

6 May 2003   *Tuesday*

I began a new regimen today in which I was transferred from bed to a chair (variously called "the pink chair" or "the Cadillac of chairs") to see how long I could sit up without it growing too uncomfortable. In the spirit of killing two birds with one stone, a therapist stretched my arms while I was in the chair. I lasted about fifteen minutes that first time, but the physical exertion paid off since I slept much more soundly that night.

---

7 May 2003   *Wednesday*

Today as I sat up in "the pink chair" for the second time, George said, "I bet at one point you thought you might never look out a window again," and I nodded "yes." I also tried to communicate two thoughts to George, but he wasn't as adept as Vicki at guessing what I was trying to say through blink-spelling. He said, "We miss Vicki, don't we?" and again I nodded "yes."

My family decided that I was on the upswing and they didn't need to keep all night vigils in the neurological ICU, although Jeanine and my mother came out for a visit from about 6:30 to 8 PM.

---

8 May 2003   *Thursday*

Today marked three weeks since celebrating the Holy Thursday Eucharist at St. Mary's in Indiana and feeling the strange muscular weakness that was the harbinger of GBS. It was also probably my best day in "The Abyss."

One of the nurses, Lynn, arranged for me to be transferred to a gurney and given a portable ventilator. That allowed George to wheel me all the way to the main chapel at St. Mary's, with stops along the way to see the overnight room the sisters had assigned to George, the Canadian Honker restaurant across the street from the hospital about which I had heard so much, and an apple tree in bloom. When George wheeled me to the front of the chapel he paused to allow me some time of silent prayer. I then directed George to pray out loud even though he was hesitant to do so at first. What I didn't learn until later was that George had come to exactly the same spot the week before to tell God that he couldn't stand to see me suffer any more and that he felt a little shy about how he'd address God in the light of his earlier prayer.

Returning to the room I had a round of upper and lower extremity stretches. The therapist told me that I now had full range of motion, just no strength because the IVIg treatment wasn't finished repairing the myelin sheathing on my peripheral nerves. My attending physician visited to tell me that the goal was to have me shoveling snow by Christmas. On that hopeful note George and I arranged with the nurse manager to buy lunch for the nurses tomorrow, the end of Nurses' Week at the hospital.

The one negative note to the day was that my friends and family were no longer permitted to give me any liquids because testing had shown that my swallowing reflex was not strong enough and there was a chance that I could aspirate into my lungs any liquid they gave me. Since I had increasingly become aware of how thirsty I was, this was a bit of a blow.

Vicki arrived about 8 PM to take over the watch, as George had to return to his Newman parish for his weekend responsibilities and my mother and sister Kathy went back home.

9 May 2003   *Friday*

In retrospect, this Friday stands out as the actual low point in my experience of "The Abyss." Perhaps it hit doubly hard because the day before had been so hopeful.

I complained to George as he left for confirmation in his Eau Claire Newman parish that I felt like I had a sinus infection. In fact my nasal feeding tube had clogged, which led the doctors to recommend that the NG tube be removed and that I undergo a percutaneous endoscopic gastrotomy (PEG) procedure in which a tube (PEG tube) would be passed into my stomach through my abdominal wall. (The NG tube was removed, but another one inserted, since the hospital didn't have the personnel to perform a PEG until the following Monday.)

This was bad enough, but the nurses decided that I should be moved to a new isolation room since I had a new infection: Methicillin-Resistant Staphloccocus aureus (MRSA) a so-called "super bug" common in hospitals that is resistant to many different antibiotics and is responsible for several difficult-to-treat infections. From this time until the infection was successfully treated, all medical personnel had to wear a gown and gloves when visiting me, although my family and friends didn't have to as long as they washed their hands frequently and did not touch any of my secretions.

The one bright spot at this point was that my new room was more spacious than the old one so that it was easier to turn the bed to let me look out the window, a recreation I grew to love. I was comforted by the presence of my mother and Kim, who drove down to Rochester to be with me after work, and Vicki who could fill them in on recent developments.

REFLECTIONS

I call the third stage of dealing with significant illness "The Abyss" because once one receives a diagnosis, the road from diagnosis to healing can be quite lengthy with few clear landmarks and many possible reversals. From the few memories I have of this period combined with the testimony of my family and friends, I think I had a profound experience of "The Abyss," "lost on the infinite sea," as Captain Edward Fairfax "Starry" Vere sings in Benjamin Britten's magnificent opera *Billy Budd*.

When healing seems blocked, postponed, or reversed, one can become discouraged, can wonder if the diagnosis was correct, can become self-centered and self-pitying, and can lash out at caretakers. Even more profoundly, one can begin to blame God for one's situation, or interpret the illness as God's punishment for past sins, or turn prayer into a bargaining session with God. I had all of these reactions during my time in "The Abyss."

I count myself a disciple of St. Thomas Aquinas in my approach to theology, and thus I believe that God interacts with the world he's created primarily through secondary causes. During my initial time in "The Abyss," however, I believed that God had singled me out and directly intervened to give me GBS, rather than believing that the delicate interacting systems of my life had been subjected to an autoimmune reaction to some unidentified bacterial or viral "invader." God had not singled me out so much as my immune system mistook the myelin sheathing of my peripheral nerves for a threat and thus stripped the sheathing from those nerves rather quickly. (As someone told me later on, "The good news is that you must have an excellent immune system if it removed the myelin so forcefully and extensively.")

Later, I passed through a period when I thought that coming down with GBS was God's way of punishing me for my many past sins. (Since that time I've come to believe that trauma can throw us back to earlier stages of faith, where our image of God is not the hard-won one we come to with adult, mature faith, but more primitive and childish images of God, projecting our experiences of wrongdoing and punishment on the Sovereign of the universe.) Fortunately, this guilt-based interpretation of what was happening to me did not last very long. I think I had had such rich experiences of God as Infinite Love and Mercy that I couldn't square that with the concept of a God who delights in inflicting pain on his creatures. (In the next chapter I will describe how I had to confront shame-based feelings and behaviors during my time of recovery.)

I do remember praying as bargaining with God. As the reader may recall, the sedation I had received had a powerful amnesiac effect, so that when I finally "woke up" I found myself in a much different place than I had been before the sedation took hold. Although muscular weakness had manifested itself when I arrived at Mayo, I was not yet paralyzed. I was able to speak, asking and answering questions about my condition and conversing with family and friends. When I "woke up" I found that the only muscular control I had was the ability to blink one eye, that a machine was breathing for me through a tube that was situated in an opening in my throat thus making conversation impossible, that rather regularly I was reminded that I could not breathe on my own when that tube was disconnected so that accumulated mucus could be removed and I couldn't take in any air until the tube was reattached, that all of my nourishment was coming through a nasogastric (NG) tube inserted through my nose and reaching to my stomach, and that a catheter had been inserted into my penis so as to drain all the urine I produced. I do remember asking God to fix the various maladies I was suffering and promised that I would live a much holier life if only he would do so. This self-centered focus in my prayer changed as I began to get better and entered the therapeutic regimen I will describe in the next chapter.

In retrospect, what I feel worst about is lashing out at my caretakers during this period. I honestly don't ever remember thinking "please pull the plug and just let me die" at any point in my illness, but George, Vicki, and members of my family all interpreted my facial expressions that way on various occasions. (I like to remind them now that my facial expression was frozen because none of my facial muscles were working, so I couldn't have been signaling a desire to die rather than continue to suffer.) I confess to feeling very frustrated when I "woke up" and discovered that I could only communicate through eye blinks and a letter board, and sometimes I think I took that frustration out on those who were watching over me.

Whether one calls this stage "The Abyss" or "The Valley of the Shadow of Death," I believe that undergoing the experience can lead to despair or a profound spiritual awakening. I thank God that his grace, the ministrations of family, friends, and medical personnel, as well as the prayers of literally thousands of well-wishers kept me from despair. I also thank God that I now have a vivid sense of the God of rescue, and I pray that this will not be taken from me as I face the passive diminishments of aging, other illnesses, and eventually physical death itself.

Suggested Listening

The composition I have chosen to express what I experienced in "The Abyss" may be surprising. Taken from a Latin text that serves as the Introit (Entrance chant) for the Fourth Sunday of Advent, "Rorate caeli" paraphrases Isaiah 45:8:

> Rorate caeli desuper et pluant nubes iustum.
> *(O heavens open from above and let the clouds rain*
> *down justice/the Just One.)*
> Aperiatur terra et germinet salvatorem.
> *(Let the earth open and bud forth salvation/the Savior.)*

Listeners may be surprised at the texture and harmonic language of this piece. It certainly doesn't evoke "On Eagle's Wings" ☺! Written for an SSAATTBB *a cappella* choir in a moderately dissonant twentieth-century harmonic language, "Rorate caeli" clearly traces an arc from the quiet pleading of the first section (corresponding to the first sentence), to the intense build-up of the second section (second sentence) culminating in three massive forte chords on "salvatorem," to a repeat of the first section, dying away with multiple requests that the heavens open. I'm convinced that the arc of this composition clearly mirrors the arc of my prayer in "The Abyss," crying out from the depths of the soul for a Savior but recognizing that salvation will come in God's own time.

"Rorate Caeli" appears on the Oregon Catholic Press CD-20612 O God of Past and Present. *Copies of the CD and sheet music can be purchased from the Oregon Catholic Press website (www.ocp.org) or at Oregon Catholic Press, 5536 N.E. Hassalo, Portland, OR 97213.*

A recorded version of the composition may be accessed at **www.youtube.com/ watch?v=5Dzp-VbU4lg**

CHAPTER FOUR

Therapy

THE STORY

Readers who have followed the story so far will probably be delighted that I now shift from a day-to-day account of my encounter with GBS to a more thematic approach to these memories. "Transition" will be the organizing principle for this chapter: transitions from the ICU to life on a ventilator unit, to full-time life in therapy, to part-time life in therapy. The final chapter will try to describe my new life post-GBS.

Transition to life on a ventilator unit

Although I consider 9 May 2003 to mark the low point of my time in "The Abyss," I remained on neurological ICU for another five days, with a succession of high and low points as I had experienced before. The major change was that the lows were never as low as I had hit earlier and the highs became more common.

The pneumonia and MRSA infections I had contracted were carefully treated with antibiotics and never became life-threatening; in fact, by the end of my time in the ICU, my pneumonia had been downgraded to bronchitis. Medical personnel noted that I had a low potassium reading, and to prevent possible seizures I was given doses of potassium and calcium that left a bad metallic taste in my mouth. I asked that the NG tube not be replaced because the tissue surrounding the original tube had become quite swollen and tender. When one of the nurses attempted to replace it, the pain was simply too intense. Once the PEG tube was inserted directly into my stomach (on 12 May 2003), the various minerals I needed could be mixed with the nourishment I was receiving. (As I recall, the plastic bags that were hung above my PEG tube so that gravity could deliver the contents revealed that I was receiving alternate foods: one bright neon orange and one a dull green. Rather quickly we named them "orange goop" and "green goop," but I could never sense a difference between them.) On the day before I left the ICU, I was diagnosed with thrush (oropharyngeal candidiasis), a condition in which a yeast-shaped fungus called Candida albicans grows in the mouth and throat. This fungus naturally occurs in the human mouth, but the antibiotics I had taken effectively killed off the protective mechanisms that maintain a balance between the "good" and "bad" microbes naturally occurring in the body. To combat its growth my tongue and mouth were swabbed with nystatin, an antifungal medication. Eventually the thrush cleared up, but not before I had intense experiences of fuzzy tongue.

Sleep deprivation became a significant issue. No matter how hard I tried I could rarely get more than a couple of hours of sleep at a time. There was a bit of disagreement among my medical caretakers, some holding that I should get some light sedation to guarantee that I would sleep, while others felt that sedated sleep wasn't deep nourishing REM (rapid eye movement) sleep. An unpleasant result of my sleep deprivation was "ICU delirium," during which I experienced anxiety, restlessness, clouding of consciousness, hallucinations, nightmares, and delusions. (For example I reported to George a horrible waking nightmare in which I was sure that waves of insects were entering my body through the various tubes that had been inserted into me.)

In addition to offering me hydration through liquid-soaked swabs and sponges, George, Vicki, and members of my family volunteered to learn how to "bronch" me at regular intervals. Given how nasty the mucus looked when they disposed of it, I am in awe of their willingness to don the purple gloves they needed for this procedure. Hospital personnel regularly bathed me, washed my hair, and shaved me. As I grew stronger, the members of my family came more rarely, stopping the overnight visits (mostly because the medical personnel decreed that I was not to receive visits between 12 midnight and 6 AM unless there was an emergency). But I grew to look forward to visits from different family members along with my mother in the late afternoon and early evening nearly every day. I grew to love hearing about the sights on the drive down (a flock of llamas, another of "banded" cows, a cheese and sausage shop alongside the highway), and the meals that they had on the road or in Rochester. Somehow hearing about what they had to eat and drink helped me participate in the experience. It also gave me something concrete to long for when my vent tube would be removed.

On 14 May 2003 I was transferred from neurological ICU to a new room: 6-F (6-650) in the Mary Brigh building of St. Mary's Hospital, in a ward especially dedicated to care for those with breathing difficulties (the "vent unit"). I began to experience the remarkable care that Mayo offers its patients, based on two core principles: the welfare of the patient and coordinated teamwork in patient care. (I'm sure such remarkable care was also in evidence in the ICU, but because of sedation and my memory loss, I don't remember it with the same clarity that I experienced on the other units.)

My medical care shifted in a variety of ways. It went from a nurse dedicated solely to my care with very frequent charting in the ICU to a nurse who would oversee the welfare of another patient in addition to me with correspondingly less charting. A variety of doctors rotating on and off of the vent unit would check on my progress every day, while the chief of thoracic pulmonary medicine, Dr. Gracie, oversaw my long-term recovery.

While in ICU both PT (physical therapy) and OT (occupational therapy) workers had visited me to stretch my muscles, but now their visits became daily occurrences as they tried to make sure that when my peripheral nerves started firing again the muscles activated by those nerves would be functional. I learned that physical therapists use biomechanics and kinesiology, manual therapy, exercise therapy, and electrotherapy to promote mobility, function and quality of life; I experienced each of these but electrotherapy. (I also learned that they [and on occasion their patients] sometimes jokingly refer to themselves as "physical terrorists.") I was frankly in awe of my physical therapists who had to adjust my physical care and challenges according to the present condition I exhibited. For example, in many sports regimens one works a muscle into exhaustion ("break down") in order to make it stronger ("break through"). If one were to do this with GBS patients, however, one could actually do damage and lengthen the course of the malady because GBS patients' muscles do not respond as body builders' do. Forcing them to exhaustion can set back recovery significantly.

Occupational therapists, in contrast, are people who help those of whatever age to participate in the things they want and need through the therapeutic use of everyday activities. Originally I thought PT dealt with the top half of my body and OT dealt with the bottom half, but by the time I left the vent unit I came to understand the true commonalities and distinctions in these two professions. I experienced respiratory therapy (RT) on a regular, but not daily, basis. I learned that respiratory therapists were trained in both cardiology (care for the heart) and pulmonology (care for the lungs). In my case, RT primarily consisted of testing the volume of air I was able to take in and blow out by means of a spirometer, an instrument that measures ventilation. The results of this measurement would ultimately determine that I could leave the vent unit.

I also benefited from the services of a speech therapist once my breathing tube was removed and the muscles of my lips and throat could work again.

While on the vent unit I constructed a new regular rhythm of prayer. Because of my GBS, I wasn't able to participate in the central action of my spiritual life, presiding and preaching at Mass. Obviously as long as the tracheostomy tube was still in me, I wouldn't be able to speak above a whisper, so preaching and/or pronouncing the liturgical texts was out of the question. In addition, being fed through a PEG tube made it impossible for me to receive the consecrated bread and wine that constitutes participation in holy communion.

In addition to Mass, the core structure of my prayer was the recitation of the Liturgy of the Hours, the formal liturgical daily prayer of the church. In its full form as practiced in Benedictine, Trappist, or Carmelite monasteries, the community gathers seven times a day to praise God through psalms and canticles, to hear God's word by pondering Scripture, and to pray for the needs of the church. The Office of Readings (Vigils/Matins) is the longest of the "hours," celebrated in the middle of the night (anytime between 2 and 4 AM depending on the custom of the particular monastery). Morning Prayer (Lauds), preferably celebrated at dawn, and Evening Prayer (Vespers), preferably celebrated at dusk, are the two "hinge hours," especially marked by singing the Canticle of Zechariah (Benedictus) in the morning and the Canticle of Mary (Magnificat) in the evening. In addition, the Lord's Prayer is said or sung at these two hours so that, following an ancient custom, the community prays this text three times a day (i.e., at Mass in addition to Lauds and Vespers). Three "little hours" (Midmorning Prayer [Tierce], Midday Prayer [Sext] and Midafternoon Prayer [None]) create short pauses in the work day to refocus on praising and thanking God. (I think of these "little hours" as coffee break prayer.) Finally, the day closes with Night Prayer (Compline), a short office just before retiring for the night, that seeks forgiveness for the sins of the day and protection through the night. Since I couldn't hold my Breviary (the book containing the texts needed to pray these offices), since I couldn't turn the pages even if I could hold the book, and since my eyes couldn't focus to read the texts even if I could turn the pages, in effect I couldn't celebrate the Liturgy of the Hours. When I remembered, I could pray what is called the "cathedral" form of the Divine Office, which consists of a single unchanging version of Lauds, Vespers, and Compline, since I had those texts memorized, but doing so frequently took more energy than I had.

What I settled on was prayer early in the morning before rounds took place on the ward and prayer in the evening when lights were dimmed for sleep. My morning prayer consisted of making an inventory of what worked and what didn't work in my body. (Notice that I developed this form of prayer after I had hit my personal rock bottom of only being able to blink one eye, so I always had something concrete to thank God for in terms of my physical healing.) Once I concluded that inventory, I posed God two questions: 1) If I never heal more than I have today, can I live productively? I always received the same "answer": "My grace is enough for you." (I want to make clear that I can distinguish between the hallucinations that came with ICU delirium and the "answers" I got in prayer. I didn't have visions or hear a divine voice speaking so much as felt a kind of reassuring holy Presence whose impact I could only formulate as "My grace is enough for you.") 2) I would then ask the holy Presence, "What are you trying to teach me?" and I never received a clear answer for that. I'll try to formulate an answer to that question in the final chapter of this book.

My Evening Prayer was another new form (although it probably arose as an extension of the intercessions prayed at Vespers) as I became more aware of the other people being treated in this hospital. I'd begin by calling to mind the patient(s) in the room to the right of mine, then to those on my left, then to those in the floor above me, then to the floor below me, then to those in the other hospitals at Mayo, then to those in health care facilities throughout Rochester, then throughout Minnesota, then throughout the United States, then throughout North America, etc. I normally fell asleep long before my prayer came to an end.

I should mention that my friend Vicki developed a very calming "end-of-the-day" prayer ritual during my time on the vent unit. A relative had sent a container of Lourdes water, which flows from a spring in the Grotto of Massabielle—described to Bernadette Soubirous by an apparition of the Blessed Virgin Mary on 25 February 1858—now part of the Sanctuary of Our Lady of Lourdes in France. Since the apparition, a custom has developed for sufferers to drink or bathe in the water in hope of a cure. As the day came to an end, Vicki and I would join in silent prayer, she would then pray, touching the various parts of my body praying for the restoration of each muscle group, and conclude by making the sign of the cross on my forehead using the Lourdes water.

A completely unexpected and delightful boost to my prayer life came with regular meetings with a group of Mennonites, mostly from the Eastern United States, who visited patients' rooms and offered to sing hymns for them if the patient so wished. As I understood it, the members of the group (which varied from about six to twelve at various visits) spent the summer doing a religious internship in Rochester and had developed this practice of hymn-

singing as a gentle way of ministering to patients. I have
mentioned earlier that hospitals are noisy places, and the
sound of unaccompanied human voices singing selections
from *The Mennonite Hymnal* in four-part harmony was an
extraordinary blessing to me since my soul feeds on musical beauty and I had been deprived of it in the hospital setting. When I first heard them, I was still on a ventilator and
didn't know if I'd ever be able to sing again, so the encounter touched me deeply. As the weeks passed I was eventually
able to communicate that, in addition to being a Catholic
priest, I was a church composer. My publishers kindly con-
tributed a copy of all of my compositions and recordings to
the group before I eventually left Mayo in gratitude for the
musical ministry they shared with me.

The low point of my time on the vent unit did not
impact me so much as it had effects on George, Vicki, and
my family. I had been admitted to the unit nearly three
weeks earlier, but my breathing muscles had not progressed
as quickly as the doctors had hoped. Just before George left
for his parish duties the final weekend in May, Dr. Gracie
took him aside to tell him that my lack of progress indi-
cated that I might have already come back to base line as
far as I would. He asked that George prepare me for living
on a ventilator and on a gurney or in a wheelchair the rest
of my life. This was devastating to George. He had had
enough experience with other folks confined on a ventilator to know that their lifespan was frequently cut short,
often because of opportunistic infections. I still don't know

how George was able to preside and preach at the Masses at the Eau Claire Newman parish while he was worrying about how to tell me that my recovery had gone about as far as it was going to go.

As fate or providence would have it, Dr. Wijdyks, professor of neurology and chair of the division of critical care neurology, ordered another administration of IVIg treatment, hoping that this time the breakthrough into jumpstarting my peripheral nerves would take place. It did, but the signs of that breakthrough occurred over the weekend when George was in Eau Claire and none of us thought to tell him. George drove to Mayo early Monday morning hoping to be there to break the bad news to me after the respiratory therapist concluded his assessment of my stalled progress. When George told the therapist that he had wanted to be there, the therapist said, "Yes, you should have been here. His respiratory functions are returning to base line very quickly and Dr. Gracie says that he will begin to ween Mike off the ventilator this afternoon."

My friends, family, and I all agree that this was a minor miracle. Even the usually stoic (though supportive) doctors were touched by my good fortune. Dr. Gracie said that he was delighted to be proved wrong by my recovery. Dr. Wijdyks, who had ordered the extra course of IVIg, said that he was sure that I would come back to base line. Most amazingly, the chief neurologist, Dr. John Noseworthy (then the chair of neurology and now the president and CEO of Mayo Clinic as these words are being written), came in crying, saying that he couldn't believe that I had had such a breakthrough.

While the events of Memorial Day weekend mark an important milestone in my recovery from GBS, the fact that my peripheral nerves were firing again brought some unexpected difficulties. It certainly caused me to confront shame.

In addition to the muscular movements in my body and the ability to breathe on my own shutting down as a result of the myelin sheaths being stripped from my peripheral nerves, my digestive system ceased to function. If I understand the situation correctly, the nutrition I had been given by PEG tube was carefully adjusted so that there would be minimal "residue" deposited in my small and large intestines. Watery waste was collected in my bladder, but because a catheter was in place, my urine moved by the force of gravity into a collecting bag that was removed and replaced at regular intervals. However once peristaltic motion (involuntary constriction and relaxation of my intestinal canal, pushing the contents of the canal forward in wavelike movements) kicked back in, I experienced a week of agony unlike any I had to that point encountered. The "residue" had impacted, and moving this hard stool to where it could be eliminated was impossible for my weakened intestines without help. Initially I was given a variety of stool softeners and laxatives, but nothing seemed to relieve the blockage. I was given multiple enemas to deal with the problem, but ultimately the nursing staff had to physically remove the impacted stool just as my sensations were returning.

Unfortunately, in addition to the pain of regaining control of my bowels, I had to confront deeply ingrained bodily shame. I had earlier grappled with guilt, understood as a feeling of culpability for having committed (a) particular offense(s) or crime(s), when considering whether or not God was punishing me by sending me GBS. Now I had to grapple with shame, a feeling of embarrassment and humiliation based not so much on individual bad acts as on the sense that I am unworthy and unacceptable at the level of being. Even though I recognized that my feelings were infantile, probably triggered from early experiences of toilet-training, I begged George to apologize to the staff on my behalf for being unable to control my bowel movements. The nursing staff to a person was deeply respectful and affirming of me (one was quoted as saying: "We're nurses—bowel movements make our day"), but I couldn't shake my profound feeling of shame, especially when the opposite problem arose in the next couple of weeks, as I could not prevent stool from leaking out onto my bedclothes. I had much earlier made peace with the fact that I would not be able to maintain basic modesty during my hospital stay, but this experience of shame went far beyond discomfort about modesty. In retrospect, having such an experience probably helped me understand the feelings of at least some penitents coming to the sacrament of reconciliation and others who came simply for pastoral counseling.

The last couple of weeks on the vent unit, I gradually increased the amount of time I breathed without mechanical assistance as well as practiced sitting up (whether in the "Cadillac chair" or on the side of my bed) for increasing lengths of time. When I began this process I could barely tolerate ten minutes, but fairly quickly I was able to sit up for a couple of hours without difficulty. Of course it may have been that I simply sought the reward of ice chips that George, Vicki, et al. fed me as a reward for staying upright. Lengthy conversations about the pros and cons of sending me to various therapeutic environments in St. Paul and/or Eau Claire, WI, occurred during this time, but in the end the decision was made that I would probably best be served by beginning my transition to a rehabilitation unit at Mayo.

Transition to full-time life in a therapeutic environment

On Thursday, 12 June 2003, I left the vent unit to take up residence in Mary Brigh Room 3-638. Within a couple of days I was moved to Room 3-640, a truly VIP accommodation where a large bedroom also held a desk and chair and a second room boasted a toilet and shower prepared for handicapped use. This room was on the third floor of the St. Mary's Hospital complex and possessed large glass windows that allowed a somewhat panoramic view of the Generose building next door. About waist high on every wall of the bedroom, mirrors formed a kind of frieze. But the most amazing part of my new residence were sets of interlocking tracks in the ceiling with dangling cords that could be attached to a canvas-like transfer-sheet placed under me on my bed. When the cords were attached to the support-sheet and the ceiling tracks, I could be lifted and transferred to my wheelchair or the bathroom at the push of a button.

Most of what I did each day fell under the areas of PT and OT. I learned how to walk again, day after day attempting to move and strengthen my legs as I gripped the parallel bars on each side of a designated walkway. I was tethered at the waist to a therapist who would position behind me on the walkway to steady me if I faltered or catch me if it seemed I would fall. Gradually I moved from grasping the parallel bars with tethering as I moved, to using (without tethering) a walker, a four-point cane, or a one-point cane to help me walk.

My occupational therapists prepared me for life on my own no matter how far I might recover the use of my arms and legs. For example they prepared me to cook for myself by having me wheel into a fully equipped kitchen. I would retrieve what I needed to make a meal by finding and moving cooking utensils, getting food from a refrigerator, a freezer, and upper cabinet shelves by using extension "grippers"; and then, seated sideways in my wheelchair to the burners on the stove, I would prepare a meal. My greatest accomplishment here was frying up a couple of eggs for an egg sandwich lunch. (I wish I could say that my greatest accomplishment was baking chocolate chip cookies for

George. As George observed in the night journal: "Kathy has had some [of Mike's cookies], as well as a couple of nuns, and no one has died.")

I am not sure what to call some of the other interventions people made in my healing process. For example, late in my stay on the rehab unit, a therapist planned an outing with me still in a wheelchair. I was taught how to maneuver my electric wheelchair through the Mayo halls (frequently banging into them, since I controlled the wheelchair's movement through a joystick that I could manipulate only with difficulty), get onto and be secured in a bus or mobility van, tour covered and populated spaces (like a mall), and journey through the outdoors with a less dense population, including wheeling myself along sidewalks and in front of traffic stopped at a semaphore. (I think of this as a form of OT, but it clearly had a social component as well.) I was assessed psychologically and given some medication for depression, an understandable psychological state in the light of what I had undergone. I was given a kit to construct a mat by manipulating the individual components into a two-color artifact. (I have it in my basement to this day.) In the last two weeks on the rehab unit I was provided with a laptop computer that I could use from my room, not only as a way for me to communicate with family and friends and get updated on what had occurred in the nation and the world, but as another way of developing manual dexterity. George thinks the funniest session I had during this period was when a very earnest therapist spent more than an hour planning with me a garden for me to plant when I returned home, a garden that George was sure I would never plant since horticulture is something I have never practiced or even been attracted to.

With the PEG tube removed and my swallow test passed, I now began to take food and drink by mouth, having others feed me at the beginning, but gradually learning how to feed myself. George and Vicki visited on the Fourth of July, bringing a fabulous picnic meal consisting of ham, chicken, and pasta salads. I was able to feed myself, only dropping a few olives and a pickle. I showed less dexterity the next day when my family brought food from Kentucky Fried Chicken for another picnic. My family members to this day can do an uncannily accurate portrayal of me trying to trap some food on a spoon pushed up against the raised side of a plate, only to have it fling to the ground as I try to lift the spoon to my mouth.

Actually, I think the funniest experience I had during this period is an event I have entitled "The daring young man on the flying trapeze." Toward the end of my stay I was challenged to learn again how to cleanse myself through taking a shower, washing my hair, using a toothbrush, etc. As you recall my accommodation on the rehab unit consisted of two rooms, the bedroom/living and a bathroom, with mirrors at waist level on all the walls of the bedroom. Next door was the Generose Building, a site to treat mental and emotional illnesses as well as various addictions. From my third floor window during the day, I could see people clustered around the entrance, smoking. On this particular day, my nurses had decided that I had recovered enough muscular control to take a genuine shower rather than have a bed-bath. To that end they put me on the transfer sheet, covered my naked body with a hospital gown (purposely not tied so I could easily get out of it for the shower), hooked up the lifting cords, raised me to about shoulder level to avoid hitting any of the objects in my bedroom, and sent me by means of the ceiling tracks into the bathroom. As I was moving I happened to glance at one of the mirrors. From where I was hoisted I could see directly over to the smokers in front of the Generose building. I was initially shocked and then highly amused to see some of them pointing at my window. Clearly they were witnessing my aerial progress toward the shower (or possibly viewing a disembodied derriere floating in mid-air).

As I mentioned above, for the sake of my health we turned away most people who wanted to visit me, directing them to the CaringBridge website instead. However, on 24 June, my good friends Frs. Kevin McDonough and Tom Kommers stopped in. Our semiannual gathering of the priests of the archdiocese was taking place that week in Rochester, so they took some of their free time to see how I was doing; they both thought I was looking good and had demonstrated real progress since the last time they had seen me. They also brought me up to date on archdiocesan news (read "gossip"). The next day I was deeply touched when Archbishop Harry Flynn, who was also in Rochester for the priests' gathering, stopped by for a visit, prayed for and with me, and gave me his blessing.

Sadly, both Archbishop John Roach, a man of remarkable talents who served as the elected head of the then-titled National Conference of Catholic Bishops and who was the prelate who ordained me to the priesthood, and Fr. Greg Tolaas, who was both friend and colleague at the University of St. Thomas as well as someone who had struggled with cystic fibrosis (CF) all his life, died while I was a patient at Mayo. Not only did I regret their deaths but was saddened by my inability to join in their funeral liturgies. Once I got better I made a pilgrimage to pray at both of their gravesites.

The final weeks at Mayo were all oriented toward helping me live an independent life back in St. Paul. After I learned how to feed myself in a socially acceptable way, George, Vicki, and I ventured out of the hospital for the first time with me in my wheelchair to the Canadian Honker restaurant across the street. We formed a small procession down the corridors of St. Mary's Hospital, stopping to visit a sister in an office on the ground floor. When I asked her what she would recommend as a specialty of the restaurant, she unhesitatingly said, "Get the liver and onions and have a slice of bunny cake for desert." I think I began to salivate uncontrollably since liver and onions was one of my favorite dishes. Things progressed fairly normally until we got across the street for the final approach to the restaurant. No matter how forcefully I pushed the joystick forward the wheelchair progressively slowed till it took some minutes to actually get through the door into the restaurant. At that point we realized that someone had not recharged the wheelchair since its last use and that its battery was almost out of electricity. Fortunately there was a chair recharging unit in the restaurant so after I got settled at the table, we plugged in the chair and planned to have a leisurely dinner to allow the recharging to complete. I ordered liver and onions for my entrée and it certainly lived up to Sister's recommendation. I also ordered bunny cake (a white cake with thick vanilla coconut icing) for dessert and had a gastronomic epiphany. The procession back to St. Mary's was much quicker than the trip out from it since the wheelchair had had enough time to recharge. Unfortunately, this wonderful experience turned into a bit of a disaster, since two days later I came down with my first case of gout, a form of inflammatory arthritis in which unmetabolized shards of uric acid invade joints, causing episodes of acute pain. The big toe on my right foot turned bright red and was so sensitive to the touch that even drawing a sheet over it was too painful to be tolerated. Readers may be pleased to know that I haven't touched liver and onions since.

Transition to part-time life in a therapeutic environment

On Wednesday, 23 July 2003, I left Mayo Clinic after six weeks on the physical therapy unit, four weeks in the vent unit, and three weeks in the ICU, and returned to my home in St. Paul. The "powers that be" at the University of St. Thomas had done a remarkable job of preparing my house to be a site for my rehabilitation by installing a ramp from my back yard to my back door suitable for propelling me up into the house seated in a wheelchair or using a walker or a cane. They also installed more handrails from the central floor to the basement and to the second floor.

For the next three months I lived at home but continued a regimen of physical and occupational therapies two or three days a week. Roman Lenczuk, my sister Jeanine's husband, kindly drove me to Bethesda and back for the first few weeks. When the therapists determined that I could drive a car with no significant impairments, I began driving myself for rehabilitation. The therapies were similar to those I had received at Mayo with increasing attention to developing fine motor skills and developing strategies to live with my residuals while hoping for further improvement.

REFLECTIONS

The term therapy (Greek *therapeia* = healing) allows us to make an important distinction between healing and cure. I understand cure to refer to eliminating a disease, injury, or condition while therapy refers to a process intended to relieve or heal a particular disorder, physical, cognitive, emotional, or spiritual. From this perspective, all therapy can be effective to bring about healing without necessarily effecting a cure. I believe that the various therapies I received from my time at Mayo and Bethesda effected genuine healing in me without fully curing my GBS. (I will detail how I assess the results of my therapy in the final chapter.)

This perspective further leads me to claim that therapy may have different purposes depending on the course of someone's illness. In some cases therapy is oriented toward cure with the goal of returning the patient to life in this world of space and time; in others therapy is oriented toward preparing the patient for death to this world of space and time and for a new life in eternity. It seems to me that our culture has developed two kinds of institutions to perform such therapies: hospitals, oriented toward assisting patients toward cure; and hospices, oriented toward assisting patients to die well.

I have been surprised to discover that I cannot identify any fear of death remaining in me. My experience of moving into unconsciousness is the closest analogy for dying that I have and that experience was not painful in the least. I do fear recurrence of pain, but I also trust that medical caregivers have a remarkable repertoire of means to lighten if not completely eliminate pain.

Suggested Listening

The composition I have chosen that to mirror my experience of therapy is a Trinitarian hymn text, James Quinn's metrical adaptation of the ca. eighth-century Irish prayer, "St. Patrick's

Breastplate." I confess to a special fondness for Celtic spirituality with its haunting combination of nature mysticism and linguistic beauty. I have also developed long-term friendships with a significant number of Irish people who have consistently welcomed me with great kindness and warmth and shared their musical and liturgical life with me.

Themes appropriate to a time of therapy include God's gift of "strength of high heaven…as my steersman," God's constant benevolent presence manifested as the "friend at my side," "watching," and "listening," God's protection exhibited in "God's shield…round me," and God's "angels of heaven" defending me and saving me from ill. Perhaps the strongest and most touching image, given the strenuous nature of therapy, is God as "Giver of rest."

I should also point out that in addition to my musical setting, this text can be sung to the hymn tune BUNESSAN, more familiarly known as "Morning Has Broken," from the first words of Eleanor Farjeon's text.

1. This day God gives me strength of high heaven,
   sun and moon shining, flame in my hearth,
   flashing of lightning, wind in its swiftness,
   depths of the ocean, firmness of earth.

2. This day God gives me strength as my steersman,
   might to uphold me, wisdom as guide.
   Your eyes are watching, your ears are list'ning,
   your lips are speaking, friend at my side.

3. God's way is my way, God's shield is round me,
God's host defends me, saving from ill.
Angels of heaven, drive from me always
all that would harm me, stand by me still.

4. Rising, I thank you, mighty and strong One,
King of creation, Giver of rest,
firmly confessing God in Three Persons,
Oneness of Godhead, Trinity blest.

"This Day God Gives Me" appears on GIA CD-807 entitled Christ Be Near. *Copies of the CD and sheet music can be purchased from the GIA website (www.giamusic.com) or at GIA Publications, Inc., 7404 S. Mason Avenue, Chicago, IL 60638.*

🎵 A recorded version of the composition may be accessed at **www.youtube.com/watch?v=yUh8i5V4ZSY**

CHAPTER FIVE

A New Life

As I mentioned earlier, I believe that after the experience of the abyss, patients divide into two groups: those who come back to this world of space and time changed by the experience or those who enter into God's eternity through physical death in the greatest change of all. I do live with a great hope of entering into the eternal life of heaven, but my experience of GBS has brought me back into this world. However, I am not the same man I was before my illness.

THE STORY

A New Physical Life

I was told by the medical staffs at both Mayo Clinic and Bethesda Rehabilitation Hospital that I would probably have some residuals from my bout with GBS, but that I could keep coming closer to base line for at least the next ten years. More time than that has passed as I write this, so I have a fairly accurate sense that my physical recovery plateaued about four years after my time at Mayo and Bethesda. I would say that I have recovered physically to 95% of base line. (Frankly, it's now becoming somewhat tough to tell what is a residual from GBS and what is just the diminishment of advancing age.)

The most obvious residual is that I live with constant tingling in my fingertips and from my ankles down to my toes. The sensation seems to be the same as when one puts an arm or a leg in a position where it "falls asleep" and as the blood rushes back intense tingling can take place. My doctors have prescribed gabapentin to control this pain. Surprisingly to me, gabapentin is an anti-epileptic (anti-convulsant) medication, but one of its side effects is to reduce neuropathic pain. I should say that in my case taking gabapentin every day doesn't eliminate the pain; it just makes me not pay attention to it, except for episodes of stabbing pain in my feet for a minute or two every two or three weeks. What Dr. Noseworthy warned about on 29 May

2003 has come true: I have suffered some nerve (axonal) damage and not just the stripping of the myelin sheathing around my nerves. The reconstitution of the myelin sheathing has gone very well, but the axonal damage (what I experience as tingling in my fingers and feet) is permanent.

The tingling in my fingertips is quite odd: as long as I use the pads of my fingers I have little or no pain, so I can type and play piano as well as I ever did in the past. If, however, I touch the tip of my finger it tends to feel as though a knife is stabbing it. In addition, my right hand exhibits quasi-normal muscular control (I'm able to spread my fingers or move them into a fist at will) but if I attempt to make a fist with my left hand the fingers tremble uncontrollably and only with difficulty curve into my palm. Thus I can no longer play the guitar. My right hand (used for plucking or strumming the strings) would still be able to play, but my left hand doesn't have the dexterity to form chords on the fretboard. I miss that ability, but since I was never that good a guitarist anyway, I don't grieve the loss of that skill with any intensity.

A second residual is that my singing voice has developed a rasp that comes and goes unpredictably. I don't have the vocal range or control that I had before GBS. However, it's unclear to me how much of my vocal decay is the result of my illness and how much is the normal decay that comes with age.

A third residual is that my gait has been permanently altered by GBS. I cannot genuflect or kneel for any length of time; when I do, my knees experience many of the sensations my fingertips feel. This problem with posture hasn't interfered with my priestly duties, although I feel bound to explain to more traditional congregations that I have nothing against genuflection or kneeling, I simply don't have the muscular strength to get up after going down. Because I also have distorted proprioception (the sense of the relative position on one's own parts of the body), on rare occasions I will stumble and trip when I am not looking where my feet are going. While I do not use a one-point or four-point cane, a walker, or a wheelchair to get around these days, I have kept all of these devices in case I might need them in the future (and have happily loaned them out to family and friends who have needed them).

The fourth and final residual is unpredictable fatigue. Without warning I will suddenly become so tired that I will need to sit down or even take a short nap in order to continue functioning. In classroom teaching I have learned to simply end my input or shift to group activities if I feel this fatigue coming on.

Nevertheless, rather than mourning what I cannot do, I prefer to rejoice in what I can do, especially in the light of the memories I have of being almost completely paralyzed. I buy the motto of the Christophers: "It's better to light one candle than to curse the darkness." As the psalmist says, "I praise you, God, for I am fearfully, wonderfully made" (Psalm 139:14).

A New Intellectual Life

I have certainly learned many things about the current practice of medicine that I never knew before my experience of
GBS. I have learned more than I knew before about autoimmune maladies, their possible causes, the usual course
of the illness, treatments and therapies, and the hoped-for
outcomes. I have learned more than I knew before about
the great cooperative work that is at the core of health care
today. From the researchers exploring the mechanisms of
illness and health, through the practical application of their
theories, medications, and appliances, to the workers who
keep a hospital clean and germ-free, health care is an amazing compendium of exact science and artful application,
raising profound questions of meaning and proper ethi-
cal activity. I have learned to listen to my colleagues in the
medical ethics fields with a new respect.

At a deeper level I have confronted, from both philosophical and theological perspectives, the question that
has plagued me as far back as I can remember: "Why do
the innocent suffer?" I'm sure that this question arises with
the intensity it does because of my experience of the illness and death of my sister Babette so many years ago. In
her early school years she developed generalized weakness
on the right side of her body. Multiple visits to the pediat-
ric neurologist who treated her never revealed the cause of
this muscle degeneration. Eventually, the deterioration led
to her limping from "foot drop" and her right hand shap-
ing into a claw. In addition to the drugs the neurologist

prescribed to control her seizures, part of her treatment was to have her siblings in effect do physical therapy for her in an attempt to strengthen her muscles, get rid of her limp, and keep her hand from becoming useless. Each evening we would take turns pushing back her hand and foot; unfortunately this therapy, while doing genuine good, was also so painful that she frequently wept through at least part of the therapy. The paradox of causing pain in order to bring about healing really haunted me, especially since, as far as we could tell, we were simply arresting her deterioration rather than bringing about any improvement in her condition. The drugs she took had an effect on her physical growth and became difficult to adjust as she entered into the hormonal surges of adolescence. After years of real agony, she successfully graduated from high school, found employment in a sheltered workshop, and was living independently with a group of other folks with some physical impairments. So it was a shock when our family learned that Babette had died with no apparent warning or reason. Her autopsy finally revealed the cause of all her suffering: she had an infection very early in her life that had in effect imprinted a groove in part of her brain. Her death occurred because in young adulthood she had another infection that settled in the same brain groove. This set off what the doctors told us was a firestorm of electrical surges in a seizure that stopped her heart.

Experiencing her suffering and death seared my thinking, tempting me to a nihilistic view of the meaning of human life ("first you suffer, then you die, and there is nothing that survives physical death"). I was caught in a classic dilemma of trying to square the experience of innocent suffering with the orthodox notion of an omniscient, omnipotent, and benevolent God. If God is omniscient (all-knowing), God should apprehend in some way all of the evil things that can and do happen in our world. If God is omnipotent (all-powerful), then God should be able to do something to confront and obliterate this evil and suffering. Finally, if God is morally perfect (all-good), surely God's benevolence would want to do something to eliminate evil and suffering. Yet our experience tells us that this world is racked by evil and suffering. Does this "prove" that God of orthodox theism cannot exist?

I have wrestled with this conundrum for decades and have never found a satisfactory intellectual solution to the problem of evil when it is posed in these terms. I have reflected on multiple ways of understanding God's omniscience (e.g., since divine apprehension of reality does not derive from the senses, in what ways would comparing God's understanding to human understanding be helpful and which would not). I have wrestled with multiple ways of understanding God's omnipotence (e.g., coming to understand the fallacies involved in asserting or denying that "God can make a stone that God cannot lift"). I have explored multiple ways of understanding God's moral perfection (e.g., can goods and evils be ranked as greater or lesser and, if so, can some forms of evil cede to a greater good, as when a parent allows a child to suffer the physical pain of an inoculation for the sake of preventing a major disease?). Finally, I have tried to make distinctions in my understanding of evil and suffering (e.g., active vs. passive suffering, natural, moral, or horrendous evil). My theological conclusion does not so much "solve" the problem of evil as point to the mystery of love manifest in the suffering, death, and resurrection of Jesus, i.e., a God who loves us so much that God assumes our nature in Christ, undergoes all the types of evil the world has to throw at him, and triumphs by revealing that the greatest power in the universe is the power of suffering, non-retaliatory, self-sacrificing love.

It has actually been a great blessing to undergo what suffering I have so that when I ponder these issues I don't do so in a bloodless or purely speculative way but as a way to make sense of my experience and that of so many others.

(For those struggling with these profound issues, it may be helpful to consult the article "Logical Problem of Evil" in the *Internet Encyclopedia of Philosophy* = http://www.iep.utm.edu/evil-log/; Anthony Flew's article "Divine Omnipotence and Human Freedom" in *New Essays in Philosophical Theology* [New York: Macmillan, 1955]; John Hick's *Evil and the God of Love* [New York: Harper and Row, 1977]; Alvin Plantinga's *God, Freedom and Evil* [Grand Rapids, MI: Eerdmans, 1977] or Eleonore Stump's article "The Problem of Evil," in *Faith and Philosophy* 2 (1985) 392-423. C.S. Lewis's *Mere Christianity* [New York: Macmillan, 1943] remains a very accessible treatment of the subject if the technical character of the other recommendations presents a barrier to understanding.)

A New Emotional Life

When I came down with GBS, I think I was a fairly typical 50-something Midwestern Caucasian male, with all the pluses and minuses that implies. While I believe I actually felt emotions quite deeply, I had early on ingested the cultural message that "real men" are stoic, that they accept pain and difficulties without complaint, that they strive to be constantly in control of themselves no matter what the situation. I found it difficult to express emotions directly, preferring indirect expression, channeling those feelings into composing music, preaching, and teaching, or poetry or hymn texts. I was quite body-denying; I would never spontaneously put an arm around someone or give someone a playful punch on the arm, and I felt uncomfortable yet grateful when someone did similar things to me.

Since my encounter with GBS my emotional life has deepened. I have become more comfortable feeling and expressing my emotions. I'm no longer embarrassed when I burst into tears at a passage of music or at an especially touching poem, short story, novel, or film. However, I'm still a bit uncomfortable when tears arise from conversations I have with good friends or sufferers to whom I minister. I've grown more comfortable confronting my own helplessness in the face of another's suffering just as I gradually grew more comfortable in admitting my own helplessness to cure myself. I've learned how to simply be present and to hand over to God the ultimate healing that will take place. I certainly feel immense gratitude to the family members and friends who went out of their way to care for me in the various phases of my illness, and I pray that God give them the reward of their goodness. I likewise give thanks for all the medical personnel charged with my care. I'm absolutely delighted that I've been able to return to Mayo a few times to share on "Grand Rounds" what my experience was as a patient at St. Mary's. I've been told by those who have attended that it is uplifting for them to hear and see a "success story" like mine since they are usually deeply involved in a patient's life for a short time but never get to see the final result of their ministrations. I rejoice that I can visit people who have been diagnosed with GBS and share with them my story so that they can know they are not alone in their suffering.

A New Spiritual Life

In earlier sections, I sketched some new ways of praying that I developed over the course of my illness. I have attempted to maintain some of those patterns of prayer as I have returned to the disciplines of liturgical life, the sacraments, and the Liturgy of the Hours.

Perhaps the most powerful change in my spiritual life is moving from a notional belief in God to a lived experience of God. Don't misunderstand me: God remains for me Ultimate Mystery, always greater than anything I could conceive, and all my language shatters in the face of that Mystery. But I have come to trust a benevolent Presence underlying my experience of illness and recovery, a "God of rescue" that I associate with the Holy Mystery that Jesus named his Abba. The psalms and Jesus' teachings have become increasingly resonant for me. Perhaps most importantly, I live with less anxiety, less of a sense that all things depend on me and my work, less belief that I am the center of the universe. I am little by little learning how to live in gratitude, more and more struck speechless in awe by the sheer fact that there is anything existent at all, let alone a universe "charged with the grandeur of God," as the Jesuit poet Gerard Manley Hopkins put it.

My relation to the church has also changed. I think up until the experience of GBS I carried a lot of anger that the church and the world weren't what I thought they should be. I was in some ways the typical romantic who had grown into a cynic because I had been disappointed by my love affair with the world. I had grown up in the heady days of the Second Vatican Council, of the civil rights and Vietnam war protests in the United States, and in the dismantling of colonialism globally. Naïve as I was, I thought if I just attended enough marches, sang enough protest songs, developed genuine community with others, then the kingdom of God would appear on this earth. I believed that the church would be at the heart of these developments, a beacon and a conversation partner with all "people of good will" as we moved as pilgrims into the future to be revealed by the Holy Spirit. I came to discover that the brokenness of the world—the stubborn resistance to God's grace, all the subtle compromises made with evil—was also the brokenness of the church—marked by incredible selflessness and love, but also marred by pride, arrogance, cruelty, and clinging to power. The revelations of the sexual abuse of children by clergy with subsequent cover-ups deeply shook my faith in the church as an embodiment of God's intention for the world. Even more painful, the brokenness of both world and church only highlighted my own brokenness, that in spite of my noble dreams there was a core blindness and selfishness in me that I was powerless to root out. St. Paul's self-analysis has become my motto:

I have the desire to do what is good, but I cannot carry it out. For I do not do the good I want to do, but the evil I do not want to do—this I keep doing. (*Romans 7:18b–19*)

Above (page 70) I described George taking me by gurney to St. Mary's Chapel. Later he wheeled me to Sunday Mass where, from the back of the chapel, I had a true epiphany: this is where I belonged, a fragile and needy man, too weak to speak the responses or sing the hymns, racked by sin, cherished by God, and surrounded by other fragile, weak, and needy sinners, crying out to the God who holds us in the palm of his hand. Thus I truly resonate with Pope Francis's call for a church of the poor with the poor, whose central message to the world is the inexhaustible mercy of God in spite of our solidarity with evil and sin.

These changes in my understanding and experience of God and the church have had an impact on my ministry. First of all, once I learned that there is a difference between healing and cure, my role as a priest became to mediate God's healing whether or not a cure resulted. It is my privilege to mediate God's forgiveness of sin in the baptisms I perform, the Eucharists I celebrate, the confessions that I hear, the Anointing of the Sick that I lead. Second, I learned that one cannot always tell the impact one has from reading external signs on other people's faces. From my own experience of being perfectly able to hear conversations carried on in my presence yet not being able to express my reaction to those conversations, I learned that it was important to linger with patients rather than to check off my ministerial encounters with them efficiently. Third, I have come to believe that most people are doing the best they can most of the time, just as I did the best that I could most of the time I was in therapy. What folks need from religious leaders is not so much thunderous denunciations for their shortcomings but words of encouragement as they face the future. I know that is what I need.

REFLECTIONS

The attentive reader will have realized that "The Story" of my new life shared above is really a series of reflections on the lasting impact of GBS on my life. So I think George should have the final word in these reflections. At the end of the night journal that he and Vicki had kept during my time at Mayo he wrote:

> George is sad that these 3 [sic] months have been stolen from us, but perhaps we have been given some things as well. We've been given a sense of the depth of caring and friendship a sense of the fragility of life and the strength of love. We've been given more time together than we might otherwise have had and the sure conviction that the remainder of our lives is very, very precious.

Amen.

Suggested Listening

The final composition of mine I have chosen to mirror my new post-GBS life is "All Who Are Led By The Spirit." In 2006 my friend and colleague David Haas oversaw a recording/publishing project to provide music focused on the Holy Spirit, especially in the context of the sacraments of initiation, because he judged that relatively few pieces of liturgical music in the present repertoire concentrate on the Holy Spirit. He invited me to be one of the composers contributing to this project and even suggested the scriptural text that should provide its foundation. I was able to complete the piece in time for his recording, and its first performance was with a group he had assembled for *Living Spirit, Holy Fire*. Subsequently I arranged the piece for flute, oboe, cello and string quintet obligatti in addition to the Assembly, Cantors, and SSAATTBB arrangement I had created for David's project.

Inspired by Romans 8:14–30 and employing a musical style like Stephen Foster with the chorally underlined phrase "The Spirit of God" in the verses deriving from black spiritual patterns, "All Who Are Led By the Spirit" comes full circle from the appeal that God send forth God's Spirit in my setting of Psalm 104 that marked Chapter One. I can witness that God has sent forth the Holy Spirit to (re-)create me, and I pray that the Spirit will continue to do so for all of the cosmos. I interpret the references to the Spirit of God in the present composition giving us "patience in suffering" and "groaning with all of creation" to be especially apropos in the light of my hospitalization. May this song inspire all to "follow where Love may lead them," even if Love leads (or more accurately, especially when Love leads) them "into the valley of the shadow of death."

REFRAIN:

All who are led by the Spirit of Jesus,
All those who walk in the footsteps of Christ,
All those who follow where Love may lead them
Are the sons and the daughters, the children of God.

1. The Spirit of God is no spirit of slav'ry;
   The Spirit of God drives all fear from our hearts;
   The Spirit of God shatters all that would bind us:
   The Spirit of God makes us children of God.

2. The Spirit of God bids us cry: "Abba, Father";
   The Spirit of God makes a home in our hearts;
   The Spirit of God helps our spirits bear witness:
   The Spirit of God makes us children of God.

3. The Spirit of God gives us patience in suff'ring;
   The Spirit of God intercedes for our needs;
   The Spirit of God is our promise of glory:
   The Spirit of God makes us children of God.

4. The Spirit of God groans with all of creation;
   The Spirit of God blesses dreams of the past;
   The Spirit of God sets a vision before us:
   The Spirit of God makes us children of God.

LAST REFRAIN:

We who are led by the Spirit of Jesus,
We who will walk in the footsteps of Christ,
We who will follow where Love may lead us
Are the sons and the daughters, the children of God,
Are the sons and the daughters, the children of God.

From the GIA CD-207 "In the Sight of the Angels" copyright
©2007. Copies of this CD and sheet music are available through
the GIA website (www.giamusic.com) or at GIA Publications,
Inc., 7404 S. Mason Avenue, Chicago, IL 60638.

A recorded version of the composition
may be accessed at **www.youtube.com/
watch?v=XLMYG8apoCQ**

I Want to See

*What the Story of Blind Bartimaeus Teaches Us
about Fear, Surrender and Walking the Path to Joy*

ROC O'CONNOR, SJ

Theologian and famed composer Roc O'Connor invites us into the Gospel of Mark to sit by the side of the road with blind Bartimaeus. O'Connor shows us how Bartimaeus sits not only at the roadside but at the center of everything Mark wants us to know about being a disciple of Jesus. An insightful and prayerful book!

128 PAGES | $14.95 | 5½" X 8½" | 9781627853279

Holy Wind, Holy Fire

Finding Your Vibrant Spirit through Scripture

PAMELA A. SMITH, SS.C.M.

How can we get to know and draw closer to this Third Person of the Holy Trinity, who has the power to transform us and give us a share in the very life of God? Sister Pamela invites us into a wonderful journey through the Old and New Testaments to catch glimpses of the Spirit at work. Reading, reflecting, and praying with this book will help to re-energize and reawaken us to the energy and joy that only the Holy Spirit can give.

136 PAGES | $14.95 | 5½" X 8½" | 9781627853170

A Deep, Abiding Love

Pondering Life's Depth with Julian of Norwich

JENNIFER LYNN CHRIST

Jennifer Christ draws parallels between Julian's times and ours and demonstrates how Julian's message of hope and joy in God's never-ending love for us can give us strength and hope. Scholars have called Julian a theological optimist. Spend time with this book—reading Julian's words, praying with them, pondering, and journaling, and letting her hope-filled message take root in your heart.

128 PAGES | $14.95 | 5½" X 8½" | 9781627853156

TO ORDER CALL 1-800-321-0411
OR VISIT WWW.TWENTYTHIRDPUBLICATIONS.COM

 **TWENTY-THIRD PUBLICATIONS**
A division of Bayard, Inc.